FREEDOM AFTER THEM

A Gentle Guide to Healing from Toxic Relationships in Love, Family, Friendship, and Work

CAIN BAKER

FREEDOM AFTER THEM

This book is intended as a source of support and reflection. It is not a substitute for professional medical, psychological, or legal advice. If you are struggling, please seek the help of a qualified professional. If you are in danger, contact your local emergency services or a domestic violence hotline (in the U.S., 1-800-799-SAFE / thehotline.org).

Names, characters, and stories in this book are composites, reshaped so that no individual is identifiable. Any resemblance to a specific person is coincidental.

ISBN: 979-8-9970305-6-8

First edition, 2026

For the ones who tried everything before they walked away —
and the ones who are still trying.

Contents

Introduction — You Are Not Crazy, and It Wasn't All Your Fault

There is a particular kind of tired that doesn't come from working too hard. It comes from a person. You know it if you've lived it: the low hum of dread before you open a text, the way you rehearse a simple sentence five times before you say it out loud, the exhaustion of always managing someone else's mood so it doesn't land on you. You can sleep eight hours and wake up worn down, because the thing wearing you down isn't in your body. It's in your relationship with someone you were told you were supposed to love, or trust, or answer to.

If you picked up this book, some part of you already knows. And another part of you is still arguing with the first, still saying *but maybe it's me, maybe I'm making too much of it, maybe if I were calmer or kinder or stronger it would be fine*. I want to speak to both parts, honestly, right at the start. You are not crazy. You are not imagining the pattern. And you did not cause another adult to treat you the way they did — their behavior was theirs, chosen by them, and no amount of you being different would have made cruelty into kindness.

That is a real and important thing to hear, and I'm going to say it clearly whenever it's true. But I'm not going to hand you a softer, dishonest version of it, because a dishonest comfort won't hold when you need it most. So here is the fuller truth, the one this whole book is built on: you are not to *blame* for how someone treated you, and you are still *responsible* for your side of the story — what you tolerated, what you talked yourself out of seeing, and, most of all, what you do now.

Fault looks back. Responsibility looks forward.

Those two words get tangled together, and untangling them is half the work of getting free. Blame is about who's the bad one — and toxic dynamics run on blame, which is exactly why we're going to spend so little time there. Responsibility is different. Responsibility is simply the parts that are *yours to move*. You can't move their behavior; it was never in your hands. You can move what you accept, what you say yes and no to, and which patterns you carry into the next room.

This matters because the opposite of self-blame isn't innocence — it's power. If none of this had anything to do with you, then you'd be helpless, just waiting for better people to come along. But you're not helpless. You saw flags and explained them away. You mistook intensity for love, or chaos for passion, or duty for closeness. You stayed past the point you knew better, and told yourself stories about why. That isn't a confession of guilt. It's the most hopeful news in this book, because your patterns are the one part of all this you can actually change — and we're going to look at them without flinching and without shame.

So this is not a book that will tell you that you were a perfect victim of a cartoon villain. Real life rarely looks like that. Sometimes you're dealing with a genuinely predatory person and your only job is to get to safety. But often it's two imperfect people, one of whom kept crossing lines the other kept redrawing, until the whole thing curdled. You get to be hurt *and* accountable. Both hands can be full. Holding both is what maturity looks like, and it's the only version of healing that actually lasts.

Four rooms, one pattern

Toxic relationships don't only happen in one place. They happen in love — the partner whose affection ran hot and cold until you organized your life around chasing the warm days. They happen in family — the parent, the sibling, the relative whose approval always cost more than it was worth, and who you couldn't simply break up with. They happen in friendship — the friend who competed with you, drained you, made your good news somehow about them. And they happen at work — the boss or the colleague who kept you anxious, second-guessing, grateful for scraps of decency.

Four different rooms, but if you've been in more than one, you've probably noticed they rhyme. The same moves show up: the criticism dressed as help, the affection used as leverage, the slow narrowing of your world, the sense that you're always slightly in the wrong. That's the quiet thesis of this book. Toxicity isn't a type of person you can spot by their job or their face or their diagnosis. It's a *pattern* — a direction a relationship consistently moves you in. And because it's a pattern, two things are true at once: you don't need anyone's official label to trust that it hurt you, and you'd be wise to learn the pattern well enough to catch your own part in it next time. Naming what they did is step one. Knowing why you kept walking back into rooms like that is how you stop.

Meet Renee

Because patterns are easier to see in a life than in a definition, you're going to meet some people in these pages. They're drawn from the kinds of stories I've heard again and again, reshaped so no one is identifiable, and one of them will walk with us the whole way.

Her name is Renee. When we meet her she is thirty-eight, successful by every outside measure, and unable to leave a voicemail from her mother unheard for more than a few minutes without her chest going tight. Her mother — we'll come to know her too — is not a monster in any way a stranger would notice. She is charming at parties, remembers birthdays, and has spent Renee's whole life making Renee responsible for how she feels, rewriting the past when it's convenient, and offering love that arrives just as Renee is about to pull away and vanishes the moment she relaxes into it. Renee has spent decades believing she is the difficult one. Part of Renee's work won't be learning that she was blameless — it'll be learning the difference between the things her mother did to her and the ways she, Renee, learned to abandon herself to keep the peace. The first she'll set down. The second she'll take back.

I anchored this book in Renee, and in family, on purpose. Family is the hardest room to walk out of. You can, in theory, leave a partner or quit a job or let a friendship fade — but "just leave" is a strange thing to say about the woman who raised you.

Family is also where the pattern was usually first installed, where we learned what love is supposed to feel like and how much of ourselves we're supposed to trade for it. If we can find our way through the hardest room, the others open more easily. So Renee carries the spine of the book, and around her you'll meet others: someone leaving a partner who never raised a hand but ran the whole house on tension; someone untangling from a friend who only called when she was losing; someone learning that their boss's approval was a moving target by design. Roughly one life per chapter, with Renee threaded all the way through, coming full circle at the end.

The shape of the journey

Healing from this doesn't happen in a straight line, and I won't pretend it does. But it tends to move through three broad stretches, and that's how this book is built.

First, **Seeing Clearly.** Before you can do anything, the fog has to lift enough to name what happened honestly — their part and yours. This is where we work out what "toxic" actually means, why the self-blame took hold, why you couldn't see it while you were inside it, and why you stayed longer than the tidy version of the story says you should have. Every one of those has a reason worth understanding — not to excuse yourself, but so you stop repeating it.

Then, **Breaking Free.** Seeing clearly isn't the same as getting free. The second stretch is about creating distance and holding it: boundaries that work because they're built right and *you* keep them, the full spectrum from low-contact to no-contact and how to choose along it, the guilt that comes for you when you finally put yourself first, the pull back in that catches almost everyone, and the real grief of letting go of someone who hurt you.

Finally, **Rebuilding.** Getting away isn't the finish line; it's the clearing where your actual life can start. The last stretch is about learning to trust your own judgment again, rediscovering who you are underneath the roles you played to survive, and — when you're ready — letting safe people in without bracing for the old ache, while keeping the standards you fought to earn.

A word on safety, early

I need to say one thing before we begin, because it matters more than anything else in this book.

"Toxic" covers a lot of ground, and some of that ground is more dangerous than the word suggests. Everything I just said about responsibility and your own patterns applies to unhealthy, draining, painful relationships between two people who both have choices. It does **not** mean you earned abuse. If you are being controlled, threatened, frightened, or physically hurt, that is not a pattern you co-created and it is not yours to fix by being different — the responsibility there is entirely the other person's, and your only job is to get safe. This book can be a companion for the first kind of relationship. It is not a substitute for real-world help with the second. If any part of what you're living includes fear for your physical safety, please know there are people trained to help you think it through safely and privately, and reaching for them is not an overreaction. I'll come back to this gently more than once. For now I only want it said plainly, near the front door: if it's bigger than toxic, you deserve more than a book, and help exists.

The Baker's Dozen

One last promise, and then we start.

This book has twelve chapters, and then a thirteenth — a baker's dozen, the extra one you weren't charged for. The twelve are mine to write. The thirteenth is yours. It isn't another lesson; it's a pledge, a short set of commitments you can carry out of these pages and return to whenever an old voice gets loud again. Because it will get loud again. Healing isn't a door you walk through once. Some days you'll feel free and some days you'll find yourself back at three in the morning wondering whether it was really that bad — and I want you to know now that the second kind of day isn't a failure, and it isn't weakness. It's just healing doing what healing does. You come back here, and you keep going.

You don't have to be sure of anything yet. You don't have to be angry, or ready, or done. You don't even have to have decided who was how much at fault — that arithmetic matters far less than you think. You only have to be willing to look clearly. Let's start where all of this starts: with what "toxic" actually means, and why the fact that you're asking at all already tells you something true.

overreaction. I'll come back to this gently more than once. For now I only want it said plainly near the front door: if it's bigger than a book, you deserve more than a book, and help exists.

The Baker's Dozen

One last promise, and then we start.

This book has twelve chapters, and then a thirteenth — a baker's dozen, the extra one you weren't charged for. The twelve are mine to write. The thirteenth is yours. It isn't another lesson; it's a pledge, a short set of commitments you can carry out of these pages and return to whenever an old voice gets loud again. Because it will get loud again. Healing isn't a door you walk through once. Some days you'll feel free and some days you'll find yourself back at three in the morning wondering whether it was really that bad — and I want you to know now that the second kind of day isn't a failure, and it isn't a weakness. It's just healing doing what healing does. You come back here, and you keep going.

You don't have to be sure of anything yet. You don't have to be angry, or ready, or done. You don't even have to have decided who was how much at fault — that arithmetic matters far less than you think. You only have to be willing to look clearly. Let's start where all of this starts: with what "toxic" actually means, and why the fact that you're asking at all already tells you something true.

PART ONE
Seeing Clearly

Chapter One — What "Toxic" Actually Means

Renee kept a list she never showed anyone. Not on paper — she wasn't foolish enough for that — but in the back of her mind, a running tally she added to after every phone call with her mother. *That wasn't so bad. She was in a good mood today. See? You make it sound worse than it is.* The list existed to talk her out of the other thing she felt, the tightness in her chest that started the moment her mother's name lit up her phone and didn't fully leave for hours afterward. One of those two things was lying to her. For most of her life, she'd bet on the wrong one.

She was thirty-eight. She ran a department of twenty people and could stand in front of a room of executives without her voice shaking. And she could not listen to a two-minute voicemail from her mother without pacing the kitchen, phone held slightly away from her body, as if the thing might go off. She had explained this to herself a thousand ways. *We're just close. She's getting older. Every family has its stuff.* The explanations were smooth from use, worn like the handle of a tool she reached for daily.

If you've kept a list like Renee's, you already understand the question at the heart of this chapter. It isn't "is my mother a bad person" or "does my partner meet the definition of something." It's quieter and more useful than that: *is this relationship actually hurting me, or am I making too much of it?* That's the question we're going to answer — not with a diagnosis, but with a way of seeing. Because "toxic" is a word people throw around until it means nothing, and you deserve something sturdier to stand on than a word.

The Pattern, Not the Moment

One bad day is not a toxic relationship. This is the first thing to get straight, and it's the thing that protects you from becoming the very person this book warns about. Everyone snaps. Everyone has a season when they're short-tempered, unfair, wrapped up in their own pain and taking it out on the people nearest them. Your father losing his patience during the worst month of his life is not toxicity. Your friend forgetting your birthday the year her marriage fell apart is not toxicity. Your partner being distant during a brutal stretch at work is not a character flaw you need to escape. If you start calling every disappointment "toxic," you'll end up alone, mistaking the ordinary friction of loving imperfect people for a reason to leave. That is not what we're doing here, and I won't help you do it.

What makes something toxic is not a moment. It's a *pattern* — and more than that, it's a *direction*. A toxic relationship consistently moves you somewhere: smaller, warier, more confused, less yourself. It repeats. You can predict it. You've stopped being surprised by it and started organizing your life around it. Renee's mother wasn't cruel every day; if she had been, Renee would have left decades ago. She was cruel *reliably*, in a rhythm Renee could have set a clock by — warm right up until Renee relaxed, cold the instant she needed something, wounded and silent whenever Renee dared to have a life of her own. Between the bad days were good ones, just warm enough to keep the list going. The moment is not the evidence. The pattern is. When you find yourself saying "but she can be so wonderful," notice that you're describing moments, and that the thing hurting you is the shape they make over years.

The plainest measure is cost. Strip away the psychology and every complicated feeling, and a toxic relationship comes down to a simple, brutal accounting: over time, it consistently costs you more than it gives. Not in one hard week — in the long run, as a rule. Healthy relationships cost something too; love isn't free, and anyone who promises you effortless closeness is selling something. But in a good relationship the ledger roughly balances, and often runs in your favor. You leave most interactions steadier than you arrived. You're built up more than you're worn down. In a toxic one, you're always paying — in peace, in sleep, in the hours afterward spent replaying what was said, in the energy it takes to brace and then recover — and the returns keep shrinking, until you're grateful for scraps you'd have been insulted by from anyone else. Renee did the math for years without letting herself see the total. When she finally added it up honestly — the missed sleep, the ruined holidays, the way she'd shrunk her own good news so it wouldn't provoke her mother's competition — the number frightened her more than any single argument ever had.

Here is one moment from the ledger, so you can see how a "wonderful" person still runs a cost. The week Renee was promoted to run her department, she called her mother first, before anyone else, the old hope rising up in her like it always did. There was a pause on the line — Renee would come to know that pause intimately — and then her mother said, "Well. I hope they're not just setting you up to fail. You know how you get overwhelmed." That was all. No congratulations arrived, then or later. By the end of the call Renee was reassuring *her mother* that she wouldn't get overwhelmed, that she wouldn't let the family down, that of course she'd still make it to Sunday dinners. She hung up smaller than she'd picked up the phone, her own good news somehow converted into a debt she owed. Nothing in that conversation would look like abuse written down. That's precisely the point. The damage of a toxic relationship is rarely in any one sentence you could read aloud to a jury. It's in the direction every conversation quietly flows.

Toxicity wears many faces, which is part of why it's so hard to name. It isn't always yelling. Sometimes it's control — the person who needs to know where you are, who you saw, why you didn't answer, all dressed up as concern. Sometimes it's criticism that never lets up, a steady drip that wears the stone. Sometimes it's manipulation so smooth you thank them on your way out the door. Sometimes it's contempt — the eye-roll, the mocking tone, the sense that you disgust them a little. And sometimes it's pure chaos, a person whose drama pulls everyone into its orbit and calls it love. Renee's mother favored the quiet faces: the wounded silence that could last a week, the comment that landed like a splinter you couldn't find to pull out, the compliment with a blade folded inside it. Different faces, same engine underneath. Learn the engine and the faces stop fooling you.

How Your Body Knew First

Your body kept the score before your mind would read it. Long before Renee could have told you anything was wrong, her body was telling her plainly. The shallow breathing when the phone rang. The way her shoulders climbed toward her ears at family dinners. The exhaustion that followed a visit like a hangover, out of all proportion to what had actually been said out loud. She'd learned to call it normal — *this is just how family is, this is just me being sensitive* — but her body had never agreed to that story. It braced, every single time, because bracing had once kept her safe, back when she was small and her mother's moods were the weather of the whole house.

Consider, for a moment, someone in a very different room. A man named Theo, who dreaded Monday mornings the way Renee dreaded that voicemail. His manager never raised his voice either. He was, by all accounts, charming — the kind of boss who praised you lavishly in front of clients and then, in private, made you feel you were always one mistake from disaster. Theo checked his email at midnight. He apologized reflexively, for things that weren't his fault, for existing a little too loudly. His stomach dropped when a certain name appeared in his inbox. Different room, different person, no blood relation at all — and the same body language of someone who has learned to live braced. This is the quiet thesis returning: the rooms rhyme. What Theo's gut knew about his manager, Renee's gut knew about her mother. The setting changes. The signal doesn't.

This is the thing about walking on eggshells: you stop noticing you're doing it. The vigilance becomes the baseline. You scan a room for someone's mood the way other people check the weather, automatically, without knowing you've done it. You rehearse sentences before you say them. You keep the peace by keeping small. And because you've done it so long, it doesn't feel like fear anymore. It just feels like *you* — like your personality, like caution, like the reasonable price of admission to a relationship you assume everyone pays for the same way.

Your nervous system is a truth-teller when your mind is still making excuses. Here is why that matters so much. Your thinking mind can be argued with. It can be gaslit, guilted, and reasoned in circles until it agrees to almost anything — *she didn't mean it, he had a hard childhood, maybe I did start it, maybe I really am too much.* Your body is harder to fool. The dread that shows up before you've consciously decided anything, the flood of relief when a visit gets cancelled, the way your jaw unclenches the moment you're in the car and driving away — that's data, gathered by a part of you that isn't interested in being fair or loyal or polite. It's only interested in keeping you safe. When your mind and your body have been disagreeing about a person for years, it's worth asking, honestly, which one has been doing the lying.

I want to be careful here, because this can be twisted, and I'd rather hand you a scalpel than a hammer. A racing heart is not proof that someone has wronged you. Anxiety misfires. Sometimes the discomfort you feel around a person is not danger at all — it's the ordinary sting of being challenged, of being held to a standard, of being told a truth you didn't want to hear. That discomfort can be a gift. So your body's signals are *evidence*, not a *verdict*. They are evidence you've probably been trained to ignore, and the work is to start listening again — and then to weigh honestly what you hear, instead of either dismissing it out of habit or treating every flutter as proof of someone's guilt.

So here is the simplest test in this whole book. Forget the definitions for a moment. Ask yourself one question about the person: *around them, and after them, do I feel smaller and worse — or freer and more myself?* Not happier in every instant; good people challenge us, and growth is uncomfortable by design. The question is deeper than mood. Do you contract or expand in their presence? Do you leave their company more yourself, or less? Do you become more honest around them, or more careful? Renee had never let herself ask it that plainly. When she finally did, the answer arrived before the question had even finished forming. She had felt smaller around her mother for as long as she could remember. She just hadn't known she was allowed to count that as information.

Naming It Without Overnaming It

"Toxic" is not the same as "difficult," and it is definitely not the same as "imperfect." This is where I need you to be honest and grown, because it's exactly where a lot of people go wrong today. Difficult people are not toxic people. Someone who challenges you, disagrees with you, tells you a truth you didn't want to hear — that person may be the best thing in your life. We have, as a culture, gotten fragile about this. We've absorbed so much therapy language that we've started using it to dodge the very friction that makes us grow, relabeling every uncomfortable conversation as "harm," every critic as "toxic," every hard-but-loving person as someone to be "cut off." That isn't healing. That's hiding, and it will leave you both fragile and alone.

Here is the distinction that will serve you for the rest of your life, and it's worth reading twice. There is a difference between **correction** and **contempt.** Correction is about something you *did* — a specific action — and it's aimed at your growth. When it's over, the person still respects you; you may feel stung, but you also feel motivated, and somehow more capable than before. The message underneath is *you're better than this.* Contempt is about who you *are* — your character, your worth, your very self — and it's aimed at control, or at making the other person feel superior. When it's over, you feel smaller, and the respect has drained out of the room. The message underneath is *you ARE this, and you always will be.* If you cannot be corrected without being offended, you will never grow — that's simply true, and no honest book about relationships should let you off that hook. But contempt is not correction wearing a stern face. It is a different substance entirely. The test is never whether it stung; good correction often stings. The test is what it was aimed at — your actions or your soul — and where it left you standing.

Picture the same situation handled two ways. You miss an important deadline and let a colleague down. The first person says, over coffee, "That hurt the team, and it's not like you — what happened, and how do we make sure it doesn't happen again?" You feel the sting of having fallen short, and you also feel, underneath it, that they still believe in you; you leave resolved to do better. The second person says, in front of the room, with a thin smile, "Of course you missed it. You always do. I don't know why anyone expects more from you." Same mistake, same underlying fact. But one was aimed at the deadline and the other was aimed at *you* — at painting your whole character with a single miss. The first is correction; take it, and grow. The second is contempt dressed up as feedback, and no amount of "well, they had a point about the deadline" changes what it was really doing. Learn to feel the difference in your chest, because toxic people are experts at hiding contempt inside a kernel of legitimate criticism, so that swallowing the poison feels like maturity.

And you do not need to prove they're a narcissist to trust your own experience. Somewhere along the way, people started believing they need a diagnosis to be allowed to hurt — as though the pain doesn't count until you can pin a clinical label to its source. You don't. You are not a psychiatrist, you have not examined this person, and you almost certainly cannot say with any authority what is or isn't wrong with them. That's fine. It was never your job. You don't need to win the argument about *what they are* in order to make a decision about *what you'll accept*. Renee spent years quietly researching personality disorders at midnight, trying to determine whether her mother "really" qualified, as if the right diagnosis would finally hand her permission to feel what she already felt. The permission was never going to come from a label, and she never needed it. Neither do you. Trust the pattern. Trust the cost. Trust the direction it moves you. Leave the diagnosing to the people who get paid for it, and who've actually met the person.

One last thing before we go on, and it matters more than anything else in this chapter. Everything I've said so far is about relationships that are unhealthy — draining, painful, corrosive over time — between two people who both have choices. But some relationships cross a line where this entire framework no longer applies. If you are being controlled, threatened, intimidated, or physically hurt; if you are afraid — not uncomfortable, *afraid* — for your safety; if someone controls your money, your movements, or who you're allowed to see, then you are no longer in the territory of "toxic." You are in the territory of abuse. And abuse is not a pattern you co-created, or one you can fix by becoming a better version of yourself. It is not yours to earn or to unearn. Nothing I say in this book about accountability, about your part, about staying and repairing, applies to that. I'll return to it carefully later on, with real guidance and real resources, because it deserves far more than a paragraph. For now I only want you to know three things: that I see it, that it is genuinely different, and that if this is your situation, the answer isn't to try harder inside the relationship — it's to get safe, and there are people trained to help you do exactly that, privately and without judgment. Naming things clearly is the whole work of this chapter. This one deserves its true name too.

Renee wasn't in danger. Her mother had never once raised a hand, and Renee would have bristled at the word "abuse" — it felt too big, too dramatic, unfair to a woman who had also, at times, loved her. What Renee was in was subtler and, in its own slow way, enormously costly: a lifetime of paying more than she received, of feeling smaller than she was, of trusting a list she kept in her head over the truth she kept in her body. She was starting, finally, to see the shape of it — not a single villainous moment she could point to, but a pattern, a direction, a cost. Seeing the shape is where everything begins. In the next chapter, we'll deal with the heaviest thing she carried out of all those years — the belief that somehow, some way, all of it had been her fault.

Chapter Two — It Was Never Your Fault

There's a sentence Renee said so many times it wore a groove in her: *I probably could have handled that better.* She said it after arguments she didn't start. She said it after visits where she'd done nothing but sit quietly and absorb. She said it the way some people say "bless you" after a sneeze — automatically, before thinking, a reflex installed so deep she no longer heard herself do it. If you'd asked her whose fault the bad years were, she'd have paused, and then, honestly, she'd have said: *mine, mostly. I was difficult. I made it hard.*

She believed this the way you believe the floor will hold your weight. It wasn't an opinion she'd arrived at. It was the ground she stood on. And it was, almost entirely, false — not because Renee was blameless in every human sense, but because the specific thing she'd been holding herself responsible for, her mother's cruelty, was never hers to carry in the first place. This chapter is about how that weight got loaded onto her back, why she picked it up so willingly, and how to finally set it down. We'll do it without lying to you, and without letting you off the hooks that are genuinely yours. Both of those matter.

The Blame That Got Turned Inward

Toxic people have a genius for making their behavior your responsibility. It's the move underneath all the other moves. However it starts — their anger, their coldness, their broken promise

— by the end of the conversation, somehow, you're the one apologizing. Renee's mother had this down to an art. If she snapped, it was because Renee had used "that tone." If she went cold for a week, it was because Renee had "started it" by mentioning something painful. The logic was always the same and always circular: *look what you made me do*. Say a thing like that to a child often enough and it stops being an accusation and becomes a fact about the world. The person's behavior is treated as weather — inevitable, impersonal — and you are treated as the one who brought the storm.

Watch the mechanism, because once you see it you can't unsee it. A healthy person, when they hurt you, is capable of saying "I was wrong, and I'm sorry." A toxic person, when they hurt you, reaches instead for the reason it was actually your doing. The hurt becomes a referendum on *you* — your sensitivity, your choices, your failure to manage them properly. And because you're a decent person who's willing to look at your own faults, you take the bait. Your willingness to be accountable, which is a virtue, gets used as the very hook that hangs their behavior around your neck.

Renee could map the whole sequence in a single dinner. She'd mention, gently, that a comment had stung — nothing accusatory, just a small honest thing. Her mother's face would change. There'd be the wounded intake of breath, the fork set down with terrible care, and then: "I can't say anything right around you, can I. I try so hard, and this is what I get." Within ninety seconds the subject was no longer the comment. It was Renee's ingratitude, Renee's coldness, Renee's habit of "attacking" her mother over nothing. And within two minutes Renee was the one reaching across the table, saying she was sorry, she hadn't meant it like that, of course she knew her mother tried. She would drive home replaying it, genuinely unable to locate the moment the fault had changed hands — because the handoff was too smooth to see. That smoothness is not an accident. It's a lifetime of practice.

Gaslighting is how the hook goes all the way in. The word gets thrown around loosely now, so let me be precise: gaslighting is not merely disagreeing with you about what happened. It's the steady, repeated insistence that your perception of reality is wrong — that you didn't see what you saw, didn't hear what you heard, are remembering it "crazy." *That never happened. You're imagining things. You always twist everything.* Do this to someone consistently and you don't just win arguments; you slowly dismantle their ability to trust their own mind. Renee would leave a conversation certain of what had been said, and by the next day her mother's version had been repeated so firmly, so calmly, that Renee genuinely could not tell anymore. She started keeping that mental list precisely because she no longer trusted her own memory. The list was a life raft in water her mother had muddied on purpose.

There was one afternoon Renee returned to for years, because it was the first time she caught the trick in the act. She'd confronted her mother about something specific and undeniable — a promise broken in front of witnesses, at Renee's own graduation. Her mother listened, then said, with real puzzlement, "That's not how it happened at all. You've always had such a dramatic memory." And she said it so plainly, so without guile, that for a dizzying moment Renee wondered if she *had* invented it. Later, two cousins confirmed every detail. But by then it didn't fully matter, because the damage wasn't about that one event. The damage was the lesson underneath it, delivered a thousand times until it took: *your memory is unreliable, and mine is the record*. Once someone installs that lesson, they never have to win another argument. You'll surrender before it starts, because you no longer trust the only witness you have — yourself.

Priya knew the water too, though her flood came from a husband, not a mother. Dev never raised his voice — he prided himself on it. He would simply explain, patiently, why her memory was faulty, why the thing she was upset about hadn't happened the way she thought, why she was, once again, "making a story out of nothing." After eight years, Priya had a phrase she used on herself: *don't trust the first version*. She meant her own first version — her own eyes, her own gut. She'd been trained to treat her direct experience as a rough draft that Dev would kindly correct. Different room than Renee's, same demolition: when someone can edit your reality, they can make anything your fault, because you'll no longer have solid ground to argue from.

"You're too sensitive" is the flagship line, and it deserves special attention — because it's the one most likely to make you doubt everything I'm telling you. It works so well precisely because it contains a grain of something plausible. Maybe you *are* sensitive. Maybe you do feel things deeply. So when they say it, part of you nods. But notice what the line actually does: it takes their behavior off the table entirely and puts your reaction on trial instead. The question stops being "was that a cruel thing to say?" and becomes "why can't you handle a little honesty?" It's a magic trick, a redirection of attention, and "too sensitive" is only one card in the deck. There's "you can't take a joke," "you're so dramatic," "you always overreact," "after everything I've done for you." Each one does the same job: it converts *their* action into *your* defect.

Here's the discernment that keeps this honest, and I won't skip it. Sometimes you *are* overreacting. Sometimes you *are* being too sensitive, and a person who loves you is right to say so. The difference — again — is aim and pattern. A loving person points to your sensitivity occasionally, about a specific thing, and still takes responsibility for their own part; you come away with something true to work on. A toxic person reaches for "you're too sensitive" *every single time*, about *everything*, and never once for "I was wrong." When a line is used not to help you grow but to make their behavior disappear, that's not feedback. That's a tool. And it was never really about you.

Why You Absorbed It

Blame felt safer than helplessness. This is the part people rarely admit, so I'll say it plainly: some of the reason you took the fault is that taking the fault gave you something to do. Think about the alternative. If your mother's coldness was truly not about you — if it was just *her*, fixed, unreachable, not yours to influence — then you were helpless, a small person at the mercy of someone else's moods with no lever to pull. That's a terrifying thing to sit in, especially as a child. But if it was your fault, then there was a solution. Be quieter. Be better. Get the grades. Read the mood right this time. Blame, as painful as it was, came with the promise of control. Renee would rather have been the problem than have no problem to solve, because being the problem meant there was still a way to earn the love. Helplessness offered no such hope.

You can see this most clearly in children, because a child has nowhere else to go. A small child cannot afford to conclude that the adult they depend on for survival is unsafe or unloving; that thought is too dangerous to hold. So the child does something ingenious and heartbreaking instead: they decide the problem is *them*. A bad child with a good parent still has hope — they can become good and earn the love. A good child with an unsafe parent has only terror. Faced with that choice, nearly every child chooses to be the bad one, because being the bad one preserves the possibility of rescue. Renee made that bargain before she had words for it, and like most of us, she never renegotiated it as an adult. She simply carried the child's conclusion into a grown woman's life, still quietly certain that if she could just be good enough, the love would finally, reliably, come.

And that's the trap folded inside the hope. As long as it was your fault, it could still be fixed — which means as long as it was your fault, you never had to grieve. You never had to face the flat, unbearable truth that this person was not going to change, that no performance of yours would unlock the version of them you kept glimpsing. Self-blame was a way of keeping the relationship alive in the only place it could survive: the future. *Next time. When I finally get it right.* Renee chased that "next time" for three decades. Priya chased it for eight years. The hope wasn't foolish; it was human, and it was the most natural thing in the world. But it was built on a lie that cost them their own reflection in the mirror. Setting down the blame means giving up the hope that came with it — and that, we'll see, is really a kind of grief.

Your empathy was turned into a handle they could pull. Here is a hard and important truth: the very best things about you are what made you usable. Your capacity to understand people, to see their pain, to give them the benefit of the doubt — these are gifts, and a toxic person learns to grip them like a handle. Every time Renee's mother followed cruelty with a story about her own hard childhood, Renee's empathy swung wide open, and the blame flowed right back to her: *she's hurting too, she doesn't mean it, you should be more understanding.* Priya excused Dev's control as insecurity, his contempt as stress, because she could always find the wound underneath. Their compassion was real and good. It was simply pointed in one direction — outward, always outward, toward everyone but themselves. You were not naive for caring. You were generous. The failure was never in your empathy; it was in who kept spending it.

Setting the Blame Down

Here is the clean line, and I want you to hold onto it: their behavior is theirs, and your only job is your response. This is the whole spine of healing, so read it slowly. You are not responsible for what they did. You did not make them cruel, cold, controlling, or dishonest; those were their choices, made by an adult with options, and no version of you — smaller, quieter, more perfect — would have turned their cruelty into kindness. That weight is not yours. Set it down. *And* — because this book will always give you both hands — you are fully responsible for what you do now. For whether you keep walking back into it. For the boundaries you set or don't. For the patterns you carry forward. That's not a burden; it's the return of your power. The fault was never yours. The response always is. The person who understands that difference is no longer a victim of anyone.

You can hold compassion for how they became this way and still refuse the blame — and I want to be careful here, because this is where your worldview and mine agree, and where a lot of glib self-help gets it wrong. Understanding someone is not the same as excusing them, and refusing to carry blame is not the same as declaring them a monster. Renee's mother almost certainly learned her coldness somewhere; she was, in all likelihood, once a frightened girl in a cold house herself. That's true, and it deserves compassion. But an explanation is not a permission slip. You can say, in the same breath, "I understand why you are the way you are" and "I will no longer accept being treated this way and none of it was my fault." Both hands full, again. In fact, the mature position — the one that honors family and truth at once — is precisely this: to see them clearly, wound and all, without either damning them or blaming yourself. That's not walking away from someone. That's finally standing on solid ground next to them.

A caution, so this doesn't curdle into its opposite. Refusing false blame does not mean refusing all accountability, and it does not mean rewriting yourself into a saint who never once behaved badly. You may well have done real things you regret — snapped, withdrawn, said something cruel in the heat of a bad night, stayed when leaving would have been wiser and let resentment poison you in the meantime. Own those cleanly; they're yours, and owning them is part of your dignity. The point of this chapter is not that you were flawless. It's that being flawed is not the same as being at fault for someone else's mistreatment of you. A person can be genuinely imperfect and still not have earned contempt, control, or cruelty. Hold both. The mature position is neither "it was all me" nor "it was all them," but the honest, harder accounting of which parts are actually yours to carry — and then carrying only those.

Which leaves the last and hardest work: learning to speak to yourself like the innocent person you actually were. Somewhere inside you is the version of you that first absorbed all this — often a child, sometimes a younger and more hopeful adult — who concluded, with the limited information available, that they were the problem. That conclusion was wrong, but it was reached in good faith, by someone doing their best to survive. When Renee finally pictured herself at seven, rehearsing apologies in the hallway before dinner, something in her broke open, because she would never in a thousand years have blamed that child. She'd have knelt down and told her the truth: *this isn't your fault, and you don't have to earn it, and you were never too much.* You get to say that to yourself now. Not as a slogan, not as forced positivity, but as a correction of the record — the plain, overdue truth spoken by the one witness who was there the whole time.

This is a practice, not a single decision, and it's worth being concrete about how it's done. The next time you catch the old reflex — *I probably could have handled that better,* rising up automatically after someone else's bad behavior — try pausing on it instead of letting it pass. Ask a simple question: *whose action am I actually apologizing for?* If it's genuinely yours, own it and make it right; that's integrity. But if you're once again reaching to take responsibility for something another adult chose to do, name the reflex for what it is and gently set it back down. You might picture that younger version of yourself standing beside you and ask whether you'd hand *them* this particular weight. You wouldn't. Over time, that pause becomes a new habit that slowly overwrites the old one — not a wall against all criticism, but an accurate sorting of what's yours from what was never yours to begin with. The blame was handed to you. You're allowed to hand it back. In the next chapter, we'll look at the fog that made all of this so hard to see while you were living inside it — and why not seeing it sooner was never the failure it felt like.

Chapter Three — Why You Couldn't See It

Of all the questions that haunt people after a toxic relationship, this is the cruelest, because it turns the blame inward one last time: *How did I not see it? How did I let it go on so long?* Renee asked it of herself constantly, and underneath the question was an accusation — that she'd been stupid, or weak, or complicit in her own diminishment. She was none of those things. The reason she couldn't see it is that the whole thing was built, brick by brick, to be invisible from the inside. This chapter is about that construction: how it happened so slowly you couldn't feel it, how the fog was manufactured, and how you came to live inside a story so complete you mistook it for the truth. And near the end, we're going to do something we haven't done yet — step over to the other side of the wall, and look through her eyes for a while. Not to excuse anything. To understand why two people can stand in the same room for thirty years and remember two different lives.

The Slow Boil

Nobody signs up for a toxic relationship. They sign up for something that looks, at the start, like the opposite. This is the first reason you couldn't see it: at the beginning, there was nothing to see. The old story says that if you drop a frog into boiling water it leaps out, but if you set it in cool water and raise the heat one degree at a time, it never notices until it's too late. The biology is dubious, but as a picture of how this works, nothing is more exact. No one turns the burner to high on the first day. It goes up a degree at a time, and at each degree the new temperature feels almost like the last one, almost normal, close enough that leaving over it would seem like an overreaction.

"Normal" is not a fixed point — it drifts, and it drifts in whatever direction you let it. Every small concession moved Renee's baseline. The first time her mother read her diary, Renee was furious; by the fifth time, it was just how her mother was. The first cutting comment about her weight stung for days; a decade later, it was Tuesday. This is how good, self-respecting people end up tolerating things they'd have sworn they never would: not by making one terrible decision, but by making a thousand tiny adjustments, each one reasonable on its own. You didn't fail to hold a line. The line kept moving, a hair at a time, so that at no single moment was there a clear before-and-after to alarm you. You can only see the drift by looking back across years — which is exactly what the slow boil prevents you from doing while you're in it.

Try this, sometime when you're steady enough: imagine describing your relationship as it is now to yourself as you were at the very beginning. Imagine telling that earlier, hopeful version of you exactly how a normal Tuesday goes — the walking on eggshells, the rationing of your own news, the particular silence you've learned to fear. That earlier you would have been horrified. They'd never have accepted it, not in a single leap. And that's the whole point: you never took a single leap. You took ten thousand tiny steps, each one so small it didn't register as a step at all, until you were standing somewhere you'd never have agreed to go. When people ask, baffled, "why did you put up with that?", this is the honest answer. You didn't agree to *that*. You agreed to something one degree warmer, and then one degree warmer than that, forever.

And you couldn't see it because the beginning felt so good — often better than good. This is the part that shames people most, so let's take the shame out of it. Many toxic relationships open with an intensity that feels like destiny: the partner who adored you instantly and completely, the friend who made you feel chosen, the parent whose warmth, when it came, was like sunlight. That early intensity isn't proof you were foolish. It's the hook, and it's a strong one, because it plants a memory of how wonderful things *can* be — a golden reference point you'll spend years trying to get back to. When people say "but you should have seen the good in them," they misunderstand: the good was never hidden. The good was the bait. And the deeper the initial warmth, the harder it becomes later to believe that the same person could mean you harm.

The Fog They Created

Confusion is not a side effect of a toxic relationship. It's a feature. A person who keeps you slightly off balance is a person who's easier to steer. Renee spent years in a low-grade bewilderment she could never quite name — never sure where she stood, what mood she'd be met with, which version of her mother would answer the phone. That uncertainty wasn't random. Unpredictability keeps you scanning, keeps you anxious, keeps your attention fixed on the other person instead of on your own life. When you can never predict the rules, you can never stop watching the rule-maker. The fog isn't weather that happened to roll in. It's a climate, and it was maintained.

The good days are what make it stick, and they are more powerful than the bad ones. If a toxic person were awful all the time, you'd leave; the relationship would collapse under its own weight. What holds you is the intermittent warmth — the apology, the good week, the flash of the person you first fell for — arriving just often enough, and just unpredictably enough, to reset the clock. Psychologists have a cold phrase for this: intermittent reinforcement. It's the same mechanism that keeps a gambler at a machine that pays out just often enough to seem alive. Renee could endure a month of coldness on the strength of one good afternoon, and she'd replay that afternoon like a highlight reel, using it to discount everything around it. The good days didn't balance the bad ones. They *funded* them. They were the interest payment that kept the whole debt from being called in.

And here is the sharpest edge of it: a rare reward is more addictive than a reliable one, not less. If someone is kind to you every single day, their kindness becomes ordinary, expected, easy to walk away from if it stops. But if kindness is scarce — if it comes only now and then, unpredictably, after long stretches of cold — each occurrence becomes precious, and you'll work astonishingly hard for the next one. This is why people so often feel most bonded to the person treating them worst. It isn't a character flaw or a taste for suffering. It's a predictable response to a specific schedule of reward, one that would hook nearly anyone subjected to it long enough. Renee sometimes wondered why her love for her mother felt so desperate, so hungry, when the relationship gave her so little. That was the answer. The scarcity wasn't dampening the bond. It was the engine of it.

Meanwhile, without ever quite deciding to, your world got smaller. Isolation is the quiet engine of the fog, because your friends and family are witnesses, and witnesses are dangerous to a distorted story. It rarely looks like a dramatic ban. It looks like your partner sulking every time you see a certain friend, until seeing her isn't worth the cost. It looks like a mother who subtly disapproves of everyone you get close to, who has a wounding little observation about each of them, until your circle has quietly narrowed to her. Priya looked up one day and realized she hadn't seen her two closest friends in a year — not because Dev forbade it, but because every outing had become so expensive in tension that she'd stopped, one cancelled plan at a time. The fewer outside mirrors you have, the more you're left with only their reflection of you. And their reflection was never flattering, and never true.

The Story You Were Living Inside

You weren't just in a relationship. You were cast in a role. Every toxic system hands out parts. There's the scapegoat, who carries the blame for everything. There's the golden child, whose job is to be perfect and prove the family works. There's the fixer, the peacekeeper, the one who manages everyone's feelings so the fragile thing doesn't shatter. Renee had been cast young as both scapegoat and fixer — the one who was somehow always the problem *and* always responsible for the solution. Once you're in a role, it stops feeling like a role and starts feeling like your identity. You don't experience yourself as "playing the peacekeeper." You just experience yourself as someone who can't stand conflict, who has to smooth things over, who feels physically ill when people are upset. The role writes itself into your personality, and then the personality keeps you in the role.

The cruelest part of being the scapegoat is that the family needs you to keep the job. A system organized around one person being the problem depends on that person staying the problem; if the scapegoat ever gets well, or happy, or clear-eyed, the whole arrangement is threatened, and everyone else would have to look at their own part. So the pressure to stay in your role doesn't only come from the toxic person. It can come from the whole cast — the relatives who sigh that you're "so sensitive," the sibling who benefited from being the golden child and has no interest in the story changing. When Renee first began to push back, she was startled to find that it wasn't only her mother who resisted. It was aunts, an uncle, a cousin, all gently insisting she was overreacting, all with a quiet stake in the version where she was the difficult one. She had assumed that if she could just show them the truth, they'd take her side. Instead she learned that some people are invested in the fog, because the fog is where they're comfortable.

And a set of loyal, beautiful beliefs kept the whole thing locked from the inside. "Family is family." "But I love them." "She's still my mother."

"He didn't mean it." "You only get one family." These are not stupid ideas — that's exactly why they work. They're the ideas of a loyal, loving person, and a toxic dynamic borrows their strength and turns it against you. Renee's devotion to the idea of family was genuine and, in my view, admirable; I would never tell you that loyalty to family is foolish, because it isn't. But loyalty becomes a trap when it's pointed at a story rather than at the actual people and what's actually happening. The belief that family is worth fighting for is true. The trouble comes when "fighting for family" quietly turns into "absorbing whatever family does." Those are not the same thing, and telling them apart is some of the most important work there is.

Here is where I want to do the thing I promised. Because Renee was living inside a story — but she was not the only one. On the far side of every relationship you've ever called toxic is a person who has a story too, one in which they are not the villain at all. You don't have to accept their story. But you'll understand your own fog far better once you've seen theirs.

Interlude — The Other Side of the Wall

Diane does not think of herself as a difficult woman. She thinks of herself as a survivor.

She raised Renee mostly alone, on a bookkeeper's salary, in a drafty apartment where she counted the heating bill in her sleep. Her own mother had been iron — no praise, no softness, a slap for tears — and Diane had promised herself she'd be warmer than that. And she was. She remembers the warmth vividly: the birthday cakes she stayed up baking, the school she fought to get Renee into, the coat she went without so Renee could have one that fit. When she looks back, this is what she sees. The sacrifice. The love, poured out at real cost. A daughter she gave everything to.

What Diane does not see — cannot see, from inside her own story — is the tone. When she told a nervous nine-year-old that she'd "get overwhelmed," she experienced it as *preparing her for a hard world*, the way her own mother never had the decency to. When she read the diary, it was *concern*, a mother's duty. When she went cold for a week, in her memory it isn't cruelty; it's *being hurt*, withdrawing to nurse a wound her ungrateful daughter had carelessly inflicted. And there is a wound, a real one: the year Renee turned sixteen and screamed that she hated her, that she couldn't wait to leave — Diane has never fully put that down. In her story, *she* is the one who was wronged. She gave her whole life to a girl who grew up cold, who calls less and less, who has clearly decided, after everything, that her mother was the problem.

She is not lying. That's the thing to sit with. If you played Diane a recording of the promotion phone call, she would hear a concerned mother and a prickly daughter, and she would mean it. She has edited nothing on purpose. Her mind simply keeps the version of events in which she is the good and injured party, because the other version — that she has hurt the person she loves most, again and again, in the exact way her own mother hurt her — is more than she can bear to hold. So she doesn't hold it. She lives on the other side of the wall, in a house made of sacrifice and grievance, and from in there, Renee's distance looks like betrayal.

There are moments, though — late at night, mostly — when something in Diane goes quiet and a different thought drifts near. A memory of Renee at nine, flinching. A sense, wordless and quickly gone, that she has done to her daughter the very thing she swore she never would. It is unbearable, so it does not last. She reaches for the familiar furniture of her story — *I did my best, I gave her everything, she's the one who pulled away* — and the room rights itself, and the thought recedes. This is worth seeing clearly, because it explains something the reader will need later. It isn't that people like Diane can't ever glimpse the truth. It's that the truth costs more than they're willing to pay, so they turn from it, again and again, at the very threshold. Whether they ever cross it is not something you can do for them. That door only opens from their side.

None of this makes the cost to Renee any less real. It only makes it human.

Seeing the whole shape at last brings a strange, doubled feeling: relief and grief in the same breath. When you finally step back far enough to see it all — the slow boil, the manufactured fog, the role you were handed, the story she was defending — something in you exhales. *I'm not crazy. I didn't imagine it. There really was a shape.* That's the relief, and it's enormous. But right behind it comes the grief, because seeing the whole shape also means seeing that it was always this, that the good afternoons were funding the debt, that the person on the other side of the wall was never going to walk through it and see you. Renee felt both at once on the day it finally came clear — a lightness and a loss so tangled she couldn't tell them apart. That doubling is not confusion. It's clarity, arriving with its full weight. And clarity, even heavy clarity, is the ground everything else gets built on. In the next chapter, we'll turn to the question that clarity always raises next — not "why couldn't I see it," but "once some part of me *did* see it, why did I stay?"

Chapter Four — Why You Stayed

There is a question people will ask you, sometimes out loud and sometimes only with their eyes, that can wound more than the toxic relationship itself: *if it was really that bad, why did you stay?* It's usually asked by someone who has never been inside it, and underneath it sits a quiet accusation — that staying was a failure of nerve, a lack of self-respect, maybe even a kind of consent. Renee heard it from a friend once, kindly meant, and it flattened her for a week. Because she'd been asking herself the same thing, in a harsher voice, for years. This chapter is the answer, and it's an answer that returns your dignity rather than taking more of it. You did not stay because you were weak. You stayed for reasons that were powerful, human, and in many cases wiser than they look from the outside. Let's give those reasons their due — and then talk honestly about the turning point, and about the one situation where the usual advice to "work on it" does not apply at all.

The Hooks That Held You

Three forces do most of the holding, and together they spell a fitting word: FOG. Fear, Obligation, and Guilt. Fear is the most obvious — fear of their anger, of the scene they'll make, of being alone, of what happens to the kids or the finances or the family gatherings. But the quieter two do just as much work. Obligation is the sense that you *owe* them — your loyalty, your presence, your endless patience — because they're your mother, your spouse, your oldest friend, because of all they've done for you, because that's simply what a good person does. And guilt is the lash that lands the moment you consider your own needs: the certainty that leaving, or even pulling back, would make you the bad one. Renee lived inside all three at once. She was afraid of her mother's cold weeks, obligated by a lifetime of "everything I sacrificed for you," and guilty to the point of nausea whenever she imagined actually stepping away. FOG is the right name for it, because that's exactly what it does — it lowers visibility until you can't see any exit at all.

Then there's hope — the belief in their potential, which is the most sympathetic hook of them all. You didn't stay for who they were on the worst days. You stayed for who they were on the best ones, and for the person you were sure was in there, just out of reach. You'd seen it, after all: the tenderness, the charm, the flashes of the person you first loved. So you told yourself that *that* was the real them, and the cruelty was the aberration — a phase, a stress response, a wound that your patience might finally heal. This is love aimed at a potential rather than a person, and it's a generous mistake. But it is a mistake, and it's worth naming plainly: you cannot be in a relationship with someone's potential. You can only be in one with their behavior, repeated over time. Renee spent decades loving the mother her mother could have been. That woman was real enough to glimpse and never real enough to keep.

Theo, whose toxic relationship was with a job and a boss rather than a family, was held by the same hook in a different shape. His manager would follow a month of belittling with one dazzling afternoon of praise — a "you're the future of this company" conversation that Theo would live on for weeks. He stayed because he kept believing the praise was the truth and the belittling was the aberration, when the ratio should have told him it was the other way around. Obligation held him too: *they took a chance on me, I owe them, leaving now would be ungrateful*. It is remarkable how precisely the machinery of a bad marriage reproduces itself in a bad workplace — the same hope, the same debt, the same slow trade of your wellbeing for the promise of a better version that never arrives. A hook is a hook, whatever the room.

And beneath hope, in the hardest cases, runs something stranger and stronger: the trauma bond. We touched on its chemistry in the last chapter — the way scarce, unpredictable reward forges a fierce attachment. Here's what it feels like from inside: the hurt itself starts to feel like closeness. The intensity of the bad times and the sweetness of the reconciliations weave together until you can't separate the pain from the love, until the very turbulence reads as passion or depth. People in trauma bonds often describe feeling more alive with the toxic person than with the kind, steady ones who came before or after — and then hate themselves for it. Understand that this is not a defect in you or a secret taste for suffering. It is a known pattern, a nervous system doing exactly what that particular schedule of fear and relief trains it to do. Naming it as a trauma bond is the first loosening of its grip, because it lets you see the feeling as a *symptom* rather than as the truth about who you're meant to be with.

Priya felt this most sharply in the weeks after a fight. Dev, having spent an evening dismantling her, would turn — the next morning or the next day — extraordinarily tender: coffee brought to the bed, an apology of sorts, a rare softness that felt like sun after a long winter. And she would feel, in those moments, a rush of love and relief so intense it eclipsed everything that had come before. For years she called that rush "how much I love him," and took its intensity as proof the marriage was worth saving. Only later did she understand that the intensity was manufactured — that it was the relief of the threat lifting, not the presence of real safety, and that a nervous system flooded with relief will mistake its rescuer and its captor for the same person when they happen to be the same person. That recognition didn't end the feeling overnight. But it changed what the feeling meant, and meaning is where the loosening starts.

What Staying Was Really About

Staying was survival, not weakness — and the difference matters enormously. When you were in it, especially if "it" began in childhood, staying wasn't a free choice made from a menu of good options. It was the best available strategy for getting through, made by someone with limited power and a great deal to lose. A child cannot leave. A young spouse with no money and small children often genuinely cannot leave, not safely, not yet. A person whose sense of reality has been slowly dismantled cannot leave a situation they've been trained not to fully see. What looks, from a comfortable distance, like passivity was in fact a kind of active, exhausting competence: managing, appeasing, reading the weather, keeping the peace, surviving. Renee didn't stay because she lacked strength. She stayed because she had the strength to endure something that would have flattened a more fragile person — and that same endurance, once turned toward the exit, is exactly what would eventually carry her out.

Sunk cost held her too, the way it holds all of us. Twenty years, thirty years, a shared history, a shared life — the more you've invested, the more leaving can feel like admitting the whole investment was wasted. *I've already put in this much; I can't walk away now.* It's the same trap that keeps people in failing ventures long past sense: the past money, the past years, feel like they'll be lost the moment you stop, when in truth they're already gone whether you stay or not. The only real question is not what you've already spent but what the next year will cost you. That's a hard reframe when the currency is your own life, and I say it gently. But sunk cost is a backward-looking accountant, and it will keep you paying forever if you let it audit your future.

And then there's the devil you know. Whatever its miseries, the toxic relationship was *familiar* — its rules learned, its dangers mapped, its rhythms known in your body. The unknown on the other side of leaving can feel more frightening than the known pain you're already carrying, because at least the known pain is predictable. Woven into this is a subtler fear: the fear of who you'd even *be* without them. If you've spent years as the fixer, the scapegoat, the long-suffering partner, that role has become a home, however cold. Leaving means not just losing them but losing the version of yourself that was organized entirely around them, and stepping into a blankness you can't yet picture. That blankness is terrifying. It is also, though you can't see it yet, the space where your actual life is waiting.

The Turning Point

No one leaves a moment too soon, and almost no one leaves on the first bad day. They leave when the cost finally, permanently outweighs the hope. The turning point is rarely the worst thing that ever happened; often it's something small, almost arbitrary — a comment, a broken promise indistinguishable from a hundred others, a single ordinary cruelty that happens to land on the day the scales were already even. For Renee it wasn't a dramatic blowup. It was a quiet Sunday when her mother made the same little cutting remark she'd made a thousand times, and Renee noticed, with a strange calm, that she felt nothing reach for the old hope. The hope was simply gone. It had been leaking out for years, and that Sunday the tank finally read empty. That emptiness sounds like despair, but it was actually the beginning of freedom — because hope for their change had been the last thing chaining her to the wait.

If you're waiting for your own turning point, I want to spare you a particular disappointment: it may not feel like the movies. There may be no slammed door, no righteous speech, no clean scene you can point to later and say *that was when I knew*. More often it arrives as a quiet flatness, an internal shrug where there used to be a leap of hope, a sudden strange calm in the middle of an ordinary bad day. People sometimes distrust that calm, or feel guilty for it — *shouldn't I be more upset?* — but the calm is not coldness. It's the sound of a decision that has already been made somewhere below the surface, finally reaching the part of you that has words. You don't have to manufacture a dramatic ending to be allowed to leave. A quiet, bone-deep "I'm done" is more than enough, and it tends to hold better than the loud kind.

And hcre is something you need to hear clearly: you do not need their permission, or their agreement, to be done. Toxic relationships run on a rule you absorbed without noticing — that nothing is truly settled until *they* accept it, that you can't really leave until they finally understand, apologize, or release you. So you keep going back to the well, trying to explain it one more time, waiting for a blessing that will never come. Let me free you from that wait: their agreement is not a required signature. You are allowed to decide, alone, that you are finished, and to act on it, even if they never once concede that you had the right. They will likely never agree that you were treated badly — remember Diane, on the other side of the wall, in her house of sacrifice and grievance. Waiting for her to cross that wall and grant permission is waiting for a train on tracks that were never laid. You can close the door yourself. That is what it means to be an adult with your own life: the authority to decide was always yours.

One more thing must be said before we leave Part One, and it is the most important paragraph in this book so far. Everything I've written about staying — the reasons, the reframes, the encouragement to leave when the cost outweighs the hope — assumes a relationship that is unhealthy but not dangerous, between two people who, whatever the imbalance, both have room to choose. But some of you are not in that kind of situation, and I will not paper over the difference. If you are being physically hurt, or threatened, or made afraid for your safety; if someone controls your money, your phone, your movements, or whether you're allowed to see the people who love you; if you find yourself managing another person's rage to avoid being harmed — that is not toxicity to be worked on. That is abuse, and abuse changes everything about the advice in this chapter. In particular, leaving an abusive person is not simply a matter of resolve, and it is not always safest done suddenly; the most dangerous moment in an abusive relationship is often the moment of leaving, which is precisely why it should be planned with people who know how to help. You are not weak for still being there, and you are not a fool for being afraid. You are assessing real danger, and your caution may be keeping you alive.

If any of that describes your life, please reach for help that is built for exactly this. In the United States, the National Domestic Violence Hotline is free, confidential, and available around the clock: call **1-800-799-SAFE (7233)**, or text **START** to **88788**, or chat at **thehotline.org**. They will not tell you what to do; they'll help you think it through safely, including how to make a plan to leave if and when you're ready. If you are anywhere else, an internet search for "domestic violence hotline" plus your country will find the equivalent, and most are just as confidential. And if you are ever in immediate danger, contact your local emergency number. Reaching out is not an overreaction and it is not disloyalty. It is the same clear-eyed courage this whole book is trying to help you find, pointed at the one situation where it matters most. I'll return to safety in more depth later on, because it deserves it. For now: if this is you, you deserve more than a book, and real help is a phone call away.

That is where Part One ends — in clear sight. You've seen what toxic actually means, released the fault that was never yours, understood the fog that hid it, and made peace with why you stayed as long as you did. Renee had reached the same clearing: no longer confused, no longer blaming herself, no longer waiting for a permission that wasn't coming. Seeing clearly, though, is not the same as being free. Knowing is one shore; living differently is the far one, and between them runs the harder water of Part Two. That's where we turn next — to boundaries, and distance, and the guilt that comes for anyone brave enough to finally put themselves first.

PART TWO
Breaking Free

Chapter Five — Boundaries That Actually Hold

Renee tried boundaries for years before she understood what one actually was. She'd announce them, usually at the end of her rope, in a voice already shaking: *You can't talk to me like that anymore. I mean it this time.* And her mother would talk to her like that again within the week, and Renee would conclude, bitterly, that boundaries "didn't work on people like her." She was half right. The kind of boundary Renee was setting doesn't work on anyone. What she'd been doing wasn't setting a boundary at all. It was making a request, and then a demand, and then a threat she never carried out — and hoping that this time, the sheer force of her frustration would finally change another person. It never did, because it never can.

I want to begin Part Two here, with boundaries, because everything else in this book depends on them — and because a real boundary is the most hopeful tool you own. Done right, a boundary is not a wall you build to keep someone out. It is the thing that can let you keep a difficult person in your life without being slowly destroyed by them. For those of you who, like me, would rather stay and work at the people who matter than walk away, boundaries are how that becomes survivable. They are the alternative to estrangement, not a rung on the ladder toward it. So let's learn to build the kind that actually holds.

What a Boundary Really Is

A boundary is not a rule you impose on them. It's a line you keep for yourself. This is the reversal that changes everything, so sit with it. Renee's old "boundaries" were all aimed outward — attempts to control her mother's behavior. *You can't say that. You have to stop doing this.* But you cannot install a rule inside another adult; you have no jurisdiction there, and a toxic person especially will treat your attempt to govern them as a challenge to be beaten. A real boundary lives on your side of the line. It's not "you can't speak to me that way." It's "if you speak to me that way, I'll end the call." The first is a rule for her, which she'll break. The second is a decision about you, which you can actually keep. The whole power of a boundary comes from the fact that it depends on no one's cooperation but your own.

Boundaries protect; they don't punish, control, or convince. Because so many of us were taught that any self-protection is aggression, it's worth being clear about what a boundary is *not*. It is not a punishment — you're not doing it to hurt them or to teach them a lesson. It is not a bargaining chip you deploy to force a change of heart. It is not a cleverly worded argument that will finally make them see. A boundary is simply the fence around what you will and won't participate in, built for your own protection, indifferent to whether they approve of it. This distinction matters practically: if you set a "boundary" mainly to provoke a reaction or extract an apology, you'll abandon it the moment the reaction doesn't come. But a boundary set purely to protect your own peace holds regardless of their response, because their response was never the point.

And you cannot reason, argue, or over-explain your way to peace with a toxic person. This is the hardest lesson for thoughtful, verbal, fair-minded people, because reasoning is their superpower everywhere else in life. With a reasonable person, explaining your feelings works: they take in your perspective, adjust, and meet you. So you assume that if the toxic person still doesn't get it, you must not have explained it well enough — and you explain again, and again, longer and more carefully each time. But here is the trap: with a toxic person, your explanation is not information they're missing. It's *material*. Every reason you offer becomes something to argue with, twist, or use against you later. The long, heartfelt case you build for why they should treat you better simply hands them a longer rope. This is why boundaries are stated, not negotiated. "I'm not going to discuss this" is a complete sentence. You are allowed to protect a decision without submitting it for approval.

Renee learned this the exhausting way. For years, whenever she tried to hold a line, she'd deliver it wrapped in a paragraph of justification — citing specific incidents, anticipating her mother's objections, building an airtight case as if she were arguing before a judge who might, if the evidence were only strong enough, finally rule in her favor. And every time, her mother would simply pick one thread from the paragraph and pull: "*Well, that's not what happened,*" or "*After everything I've done, this is how you talk to me?*" — and within minutes Renee was defending her evidence instead of keeping her boundary, dragged back onto the old battlefield where her mother always won. The day Renee finally said only, "That doesn't work for me," and refused to add a single sentence more, her mother was visibly thrown. There was nothing to grab. An explanation is a handhold; a boundary offered without one is a smooth wall. It felt rude to Renee at first, almost cruel, to withhold the reasons she'd always felt obligated to provide. It wasn't cruel. It was the first time she'd stopped handing over the rope.

Building Ones That Stick

A boundary that sticks is clear, specific, and about your own action — never a vague plea about theirs. "I need you to respect me" is not a boundary; it's a wish, and an unmeasurable one. A boundary names a specific behavior and a specific response you control. *If you raise your voice at me, I'm going to leave and we'll try again another day. If you comment on my weight, I'll change the subject, and if it continues, I'll head home.* Notice the shape: a concrete trigger, and then your action — leave, hang up, change the subject, go home. Nothing in it requires the other person to agree, understand, or cooperate. Renee's turning point with boundaries came when she stopped writing rules for her mother and started writing scripts for herself: not "Mom, you need to stop," but a quiet inner plan for exactly what she would do the next time the line was crossed. The first had failed for thirty years. The second worked within a month, because it was the only kind that was ever hers to enforce.

The consequence is the boundary. The follow-through is the entire thing. A boundary you don't enforce isn't a boundary; it's a suggestion, and toxic people are exquisitely sensitive to the difference. If you say you'll leave when the yelling starts and then you stay, you haven't set a boundary — you've taught them precisely how much yelling it takes to make you fold, which is worse than saying nothing. This is the part that separates people who "keep trying boundaries" from people who are finally free: the willingness to actually do the thing. The first time Renee calmly said, "I'm going to go now, we can talk another time," and then *hung up the phone* while her mother was still going — not in anger, just with finality — something shifted that no speech ever had. She hadn't controlled her mother. She'd simply demonstrated, through action rather than words, that the old behavior no longer bought the old access. The follow-through is not the enforcement of the boundary. It *is* the boundary. Everything before it is just talk.

Sometimes the most powerful move is to stop feeding the drama at all — what people call "gray rock." Marcus discovered this with a friend who ran his life on manufactured crises. Every conversation was an emergency, every emergency required Marcus to drop everything, and any hesitation was met with a wounded speech about loyalty. Marcus couldn't reason his friend out of it, and he wasn't ready to end a twenty-year friendship. So he tried something quieter: he became boring. He stopped supplying the big emotional reactions the drama fed on — no gasping, no long counsel, no rescue. Just calm, brief, unbothered responses. *Huh. That sounds hard. Hope it works out.* Deprived of the reaction it existed to provoke, the drama slowly lost interest in him. Gray rock isn't coldness for its own sake, and it isn't a trick to punish someone; it's disengagement from a specific game you keep losing. You don't have to win the argument or attend the crisis. Sometimes you just decline to play, and the game cannot continue without you.

It's worth being honest about what happened next for Marcus, because it shows both the power and the limit of the tool. With less fuel, the friendship got quieter — fewer 2 a.m. emergencies, fewer guilt speeches — and for a while Marcus thought he'd found the answer that let him keep his friend without the chaos. But he also noticed something a little sad: once he stopped supplying rescue, there wasn't much friendship left underneath. The relationship, it turned out, had been almost entirely built on his role as first responder. Gray rock had revealed the truth rather than fixed it. That's often how it goes. Disengagement is excellent for surviving a difficult person you can't or don't want to leave — a coworker, a co-parent, an in-law you'll see at every holiday. It is a way to stay in the room without bleeding. What it cannot do is manufacture a real connection where the raw materials were never there. Sometimes the boundary keeps the relationship. Sometimes it shows you what the relationship actually was.

Holding the Line Under Pressure

When you first hold a boundary, expect it to get worse before it gets better. This is so predictable it has a name: the extinction burst. Think of a child who has learned that a tantrum in the store gets them candy. The day you finally stop giving in, the tantrum doesn't shrink — it explodes, louder and longer than ever, because escalation has always worked before and the child is, quite reasonably, trying harder. A toxic adult does exactly the same thing. The first few times your boundary holds, the pushback will intensify: more guilt, more rage, more charm, more crisis, whatever has moved you in the past, now turned up to full volume. Most people read this spike as proof the boundary is failing and backing them into disaster, and they cave — which teaches the other person that escalation still works, and the whole thing gets harder next time. But the burst is not a sign of failure. It is a sign that the boundary is *working*, that the old lever is being frantically yanked because it's stopped delivering. If you can hold through the burst without flinching, it almost always subsides. The trouble is that the burst is engineered, precisely, to make you flinch.

When Renee first started hanging up on cruelty, the escalation was frightening. Her mother, who had never been one for grand scenes, suddenly produced them: a flurry of increasingly wounded voicemails, a tearful message about her health, then a cold one about Renee's selfishness, then an aunt calling to say her mother was "beside herself" and how could Renee do this to her. It felt like the sky falling, exactly as it was meant to. Every instinct screamed that she'd gone too far, broken something, caused real harm — that the decent thing was to call back and smooth it all over. She very nearly did. What stopped her was recognizing the pattern for what it was: not a catastrophe she'd caused, but a burst she'd triggered by finally not folding. She waited. Within about two weeks, the storm simply passed, and her mother resumed contact as if none of it had happened — calmer, and, tellingly, a shade more careful. The burst had been the last, loudest attempt to work a lever that no longer moved anything. Knowing it was coming was what let Renee survive it. If you brace for the burst as a normal, expected stage rather than an emergency, you rob it of most of its power.

Guilt-trips, rage, and tears are not spontaneous emotions in these moments. They are tests. I say this carefully, because sometimes tears are real and pain is genuine, and a loving person's hurt at a boundary deserves your tenderness. But in a toxic dynamic, watch what the "hurt" is *for*. If every time you hold a line the other person produces exactly the emotion most likely to make you drop it — the sobbing when you're softhearted, the fury when you're conflict-averse, the sudden warmth when you're starved for it — you are not witnessing feelings so much as watching a set of keys being tried in a lock. The response to a test is not to argue with it or to prove you're not heartless. It's to stay warm and stay put: *I can see you're upset, and I'm still going to head home.* You don't have to match their intensity, defend your reasoning, or win. You only have to not pick the lock open for them. Kindness and firmness are not opposites; the strongest boundary is held with a steady, almost gentle calm.

And underneath all of it, the permission you most need to grant yourself: you are allowed to protect your peace, even from people you love. This is where so many good-hearted people falter, because they've absorbed the idea that love means limitless availability, that a real daughter or a true friend endures anything. But there is nothing loving, to you or to them, in offering yourself up to be worn down. A boundary is not a withdrawal of love; very often it's what makes continued love possible, the fence that lets you stay near someone without being trampled. Renee did not stop loving her mother when she started hanging up on cruelty. In a strange way she loved her more cleanly, because she was no longer drowning in resentment, no longer forced to choose between self-respect and the relationship. That is the quiet promise of boundaries, and the reason they open Part Two: they are how you break free from the *dynamic* without necessarily breaking from the *person*. For some relationships, boundaries will be enough, and you'll get to keep the person on livable terms. For others, you'll find the boundaries can't hold no matter how well you build them, because the other person will not allow any version of you that has them — and that harder possibility, the question of distance, is where the next chapter goes.

Chapter Six — Creating Distance: Low-Contact and No-Contact

When people imagine getting free of a toxic family member, they usually picture one dramatic act: the door slammed forever, the number blocked, the person erased. And because that picture is so extreme, so final, so much like a bomb going off in the middle of a family, most people recoil from it — *I could never do that, she's still my mother* — and conclude that their only other option is to keep enduring exactly as before. This is a false choice, and it traps more people than almost anything else in this book. Between "endure it all" and "cut them off completely" lies an enormous, underused middle, and learning to live in that middle is the whole art of this chapter. I want to say clearly, before we begin, where I stand: I am not here to talk you into cutting off your family. I believe in staying and working at the people who matter, and I think our age reaches for estrangement far too quickly and calls the resulting quiet "peace." But I also refuse to lie to you about the cases where distance is the only sane response left. So we're going to hold both truths at once, and let you find the honest setting for your own situation.

The Distance Spectrum

Distance is a dial, not a switch. This is the single most important idea in the chapter, so let it replace the slammed-door picture entirely. On one end of the dial is full, open contact; on the other is no contact at all. But almost all of the useful territory is in between: seeing someone less often, keeping conversations to safe topics, declining to attend certain events, taking a season's pause, meeting only in certain settings. The goal is not to crank the dial to maximum distance. The goal is to turn it the *least* amount that lets you breathe — and no further. Most people never discover the middle settings, because no one told them the dial existed. They think it's endure or annihilate. It isn't. For the great majority of difficult relationships, some modest, sustainable turn of the dial is all that's required, and the relationship survives in a form you can actually live with.

Sometimes, though, distance is the only boundary a toxic person will respect. Here is the hard mechanism you may have already run into: a boundary only works if the other person will honor your control of your own actions. But some people treat every boundary as a wall to be climbed. You say you'll leave if they yell; they follow you to the car. You limit the topics; they ambush you with them anyway. You ask for space; they show up unannounced. When someone will not respect any line you hold while in contact, then reducing contact *becomes* the boundary — the only one left that doesn't depend on their cooperation. Distance, in that case, is not you failing at boundaries. It is you enforcing one in the only way that remains available. You turned the dial not because you wanted to, but because they left you nothing nearer that held.

I know that some readers will feel, at this point, the same resistance I feel — that stepping back looks like *running,* like abandoning the harder, nobler work of staying and fighting for the relationship. I share that instinct, so let me answer it directly. There is a world of difference between running from a fight and recognizing there is no fight to be had. A fight, in the honorable sense, requires two people willing to fight *fair* — to hear each other, to give ground, to want repair as much as victory. You cannot fight for a family that only fights to win. When the other person treats every attempt at repair as ammunition, refuses every olive branch, and returns your good-faith effort with contempt, then what you're calling a fight is not a fight at all. It's a beating that you keep showing up for and calling loyalty. Stepping back from that is not cowardice. It's the sober recognition that the thing you were willing to fight *for* requires a partner who was never in the ring.

And no-contact, when it genuinely comes to that, is not hatred. Often it's a tourniquet. You don't apply a tourniquet because you hate the limb. You apply it because you're bleeding out and nothing gentler has stopped it. No-contact is the same: an emergency measure to stop a wound that won't close any other way. Two things follow from that image, and both matter. First, a tourniquet is not necessarily forever — sometimes distance is a temporary measure that lets you heal enough to one day re-approach on new terms, and a season of no-contact can even be what makes an eventual, healthier reconnection possible. Second, a tourniquet is not applied lightly or first; you reach for it when the bleeding is severe and other measures have failed. That is exactly the spirit in which I want you to hold no-contact: not as a first move, not as a trend, not as the fashionable way to announce you've done your inner work — but as a serious, sometimes life-saving last resort, taken soberly, and sometimes only for a time.

And because I've been firm that distance should be the last setting you reach for, I have to be just as firm about the exception, or I'd be doing you a quiet disservice. For some people, the far end of the dial is not the last resort — it's the right *first* move. If a parent, partner, or relative is genuinely dangerous — violent, threatening, or so relentlessly destructive that mere proximity is harm — then the graduated approach I've described does not apply, and no one should tell you to keep "trying the middle settings" with someone who is hurting you. There, distance isn't the failure of repair; it's survival, and it may need to come fast and be planned carefully, since, as we saw earlier, leaving can be the most dangerous moment of all. Consider Daniel, whose father's rage had put him in the hospital more than once as a boy and never softened with the years. Daniel didn't owe that man a graduated spectrum of chances. He went no-contact in his twenties, cleanly and permanently, and it was one of the healthiest decisions of his life. When people who knew only the charming public version murmured that he should reconcile because "that's your father," Daniel had a quiet, unshakable answer: a title is not a free pass, and blood does not obligate you to bleed. His no-contact was not the cultural reflex I've been warning against. It was a grown man refusing to hand his own children a grandfather who might harm them too. Both things are true at once — that we cut off too easily as a culture, *and* that some cutoffs are entirely, unarguably right. Wisdom is knowing which situation is actually yours, and being brutally honest with yourself about it.

Doing It With Care

The most repair-friendly setting on the dial is structured contact, and it's where Renee landed. She did not cut off her mother. The thought of it made her ill, and more to the point, it wasn't what she wanted — she wanted a mother, or at least the most livable version of one available. So she built a structure instead. She saw her mother in public places, where the worst behavior tended to stay leashed. She kept visits time-boxed — a lunch, not a weekend — so there was always a natural, non-dramatic end. When she could, she brought a witness: her husband, a cousin, someone whose mere presence changed the temperature. And she chose the topics she'd engage and the ones she'd simply let slide past. It was not the warm, open mother-daughter bond she'd once dreamed of. But it was real contact, sustainable and mostly peaceful, and it let her keep her mother in her life without being flattened by her. For a great many of you, this — not no-contact — is the actual destination: a downshifted, structured, clear-eyed relationship that you get to keep.

The logistics are where good intentions live or die, so think them through in advance. Distance has a hundred practical seams where the old dynamic tries to sneak back in — the holidays, the group chat, the shared friends, the aging parent who needs care, the sibling's wedding. Decide these in calm moments, not ambushed in the doorway. What will you do at holidays: attend for a fixed window, host on your own terms, or opt out and plan something restorative instead? How will you handle messages — reply on your own schedule, keep it brief, let some go unanswered? What will you say to the shared people who carry news back and forth? And if there's caretaking to be shared, how much can you give through logistics and money rather than through the exposure that costs you most? None of this has one right answer. The point is that you author the terms deliberately, rather than letting the relationship's old gravity decide them for you by default.

If it does come to no-contact, there is a clean way to do it — and sometimes the cleanest thing is silence. You do not owe a toxic person a final speech that lays out every grievance; that letter is almost always for you, not them, and it usually just hands them fresh material. If you choose to say something, keep it short, calm, and free of arguments to rebut: *I need to step back from our relationship. I'm not going to discuss it, and I wish you well.* No case, no evidence, no opening for negotiation. And often the better choice is to send nothing at all — to simply, quietly, let the contact end without a starting gun that invites a siege. Silence is not cowardice here. A person who has spent years turning your words against you has not earned a closing statement. You are allowed to close the door softly and walk away without narrating it.

The Fallout to Expect

Expect the flying monkeys. It's a strange phrase, borrowed from the winged servants the witch sends in the old story, but anyone who has created distance from a toxic person knows exactly what it names: the relatives and mutual friends who suddenly appear, dispatched to guilt you back into line. *Your mother is heartbroken. After everything she's done for you. Family is family. You're being cruel.* Some of them are knowing accomplices; most are simply well-meaning people who've been fed a one-sided story and genuinely believe they're helping. Either way, their arrival is not evidence that you're wrong. It's evidence that the system is trying to restore itself, because your distance has disturbed an arrangement everyone else had grown comfortable with. You do not have to argue with the flying monkeys or win them over. "I understand you're worried, and this is between me and her" is enough, repeated as often as needed, and then not defended further.

Expect, too, the story they will tell about you — the smear campaign. This one wounds deeply, because it attacks the very thing that made you vulnerable: your desire to be seen as good. A toxic person, faced with your distance, will very often get their version out first — the ungrateful child, the crazy ex, the difficult one who abandoned poor them — and it can travel through a family or a friend group like a grease fire. It helps to know this in advance, so it lands as a predictable move rather than a fresh betrayal. It helps more to accept a hard freedom: you cannot control the narrative, and trying to correct it to every listener will only exhaust you and make you look exactly as unhinged as the story claims. The people who truly know you will, in time, weigh the story against the person they've always known. The ones who swallow it whole were never really yours to lose. Let the truth be slow. It usually is, and it usually wins.

Through all of it, protect your energy and your circle while the dust settles. Creating distance, even when it's plainly right, kicks up grief and doubt and a peculiar loneliness, and the fallout can tempt you to either isolate completely or race back to make it stop. Do neither. This is precisely when you lean toward the good people, not away from them — and here I'll say the thing I most want you to carry out of this chapter. The purpose of distance is never solitude. I don't believe there's any peace to be found in cutting yourself off from everyone and calling the silence serenity. The purpose of putting distance between you and a corrosive relationship is to *protect your capacity for all the others* — to stop pouring your finite self into a bucket with a hole in it, so you have something left for the friends, the partner, the children, the family members who actually love you back. You are not walking away from connection. You are walling off the one drain so the rest of the garden can finally get water. Keep that straight, and distance stops feeling like exile and starts feeling like what it is: the clearing of room. In the next chapter, we'll deal with the heaviest thing the fallout stirs up — not what others say about your choice, but the guilt that rises from inside you, and how to tell the guilt that's teaching you something from the guilt that was installed to keep you in line.

Chapter Seven — The Guilt of Walking Away

The distance was the easy part. That surprised Renee. She had braced for the logistics of pulling back to be the hard thing, and instead the hard thing was what happened *inside* her afterward — the guilt that arrived like a tide the moment the house went quiet, whispering that she was selfish, that she'd abandoned her own mother, that one day she'd stand at a graveside sick with regret. The guilt was so physical, so certain, that it felt like a verdict. And this is where a great many people, having done the brave and difficult work of stepping back, quietly undo all of it — not because the distance was wrong, but because the guilt was unbearable. So this chapter is about the guilt: where it comes from, which parts of it are worth listening to and which were installed to control you, and how to make a durable peace with a choice your own conscience keeps putting on trial.

The Weaponized "Family"

"But they're your mother." Let's take that sentence seriously, because it's usually used to end thinking rather than to do any. I want to be careful here, because I actually believe family means something. I don't think obligations to the people who raised us are imaginary, and I have no patience for the idea that we owe our parents nothing. Family is a real bond with real weight, and honoring it is a genuine good. But notice how that true and worthy sentiment gets used. "They're your mother" is deployed not to remind you of a real bond you'd forgotten, but to override your own experience — to say that the *title* cancels the *treatment*, that the role comes with an unlimited line of credit no behavior can overdraw. And that simply isn't true. Honoring your mother has never meant submitting to harm from her. The obligation family carries is real, but it is not infinite, and it was never meant to be a chain that binds you to your own diminishment. You can hold family sacred and still refuse to let the word be used as a bludgeon.

Renee got the full sermon from an aunt over coffee, six months into keeping her distance. "She's your *mother*, Renee. You only get one. She won't be around forever, and you'll have to live with how you treated her." Every sentence was true in the abstract, and every sentence was aimed at a single target: getting Renee to abandon her own hard-won limits and return to full, unguarded contact. What her aunt never once asked was how her mother had treated *her* — that half of the ledger simply didn't exist in the conversation. Renee noticed something important that afternoon. The people who lean hardest on "family is family" are almost always asking you to absorb, forgive, and show up; they are almost never asking the difficult family member to stop doing the thing that drove you away. The obligation, in their telling, only ever runs one direction. A bond that real would run both ways, and the fact that it's only ever invoked to pull you back toward harm tells you it's being used as leverage, not honored as love.

Watch, too, for forced forgiveness and the gospel of "keeping the peace." You'll be told to forgive, to let it go, to stop dwelling, to be the bigger person — often by people who've never had to live it. Now, forgiveness is a real and often beautiful thing, and I won't cheapen it by pretending it's always a trap; releasing a grievance can free the one who carries it, and sometimes that person is you. But forgiveness has been counterfeited, and the counterfeit is everywhere. Real forgiveness is something you may arrive at, in your own time, for your own peace, and it costs the other person nothing and grants them no automatic return of access. The counterfeit is a demand — *forgive now, on their terms, and prove it by pretending it never happened and letting them back in.* That's not forgiveness; it's a reset button that restores the old machine. "Keeping the peace" is the same counterfeit wearing a calmer face: what's usually being kept is not peace but *quiet,* and the quiet is purchased entirely with your silence. A peace that requires only you to keep swallowing things is not peace. It's a ceasefire in a war only one side ever agreed to stop fighting.

This is the right place to say plainly where estrangement belongs: it is a last resort, not a first move — and it can still be exactly right. I've argued throughout this book that we reach for cutting people off too readily, and I stand by that. Estrangement should come after the boundaries, the distance, the honest attempts at repair — not before them, and not as an opening bid. That's the discipline. But discipline is not the same as prohibition, and I would be lying to you if I said a last resort is never needed. Sometimes every nearer option has genuinely been exhausted, and the only remaining choice is between the relationship and yourself. When it truly comes to that — when you've actually done the work and the other person has answered every effort with more harm — then estrangement is not a failure of loyalty. It's loyalty finally, rightly, turned toward the person who also deserves it: you. Both things stay true. Don't reach for the last resort first. And don't let anyone shame you out of it when it's genuinely the last resort you have left.

Whose Voice Is the Guilt?

Most of the guilt you feel is borrowed — it speaks in a voice that was installed in you, and it isn't always yours. When Renee felt that tide of guilt, she assumed it was her own conscience delivering a true verdict. But when she listened closely to the actual words, she recognized them: *you're selfish, you're ungrateful, after everything I've done, how could you.* That wasn't the voice of Renee's conscience. It was her mother's voice, and her aunt's, and the whole family chorus, playing back inside her own head long after she'd stopped picking up the phone. This is one of the cruelest tricks of a toxic upbringing: the judge gets installed internally, so that the other person no longer has to punish you — you'll do it for them, automatically, for free, forever. Learning to ask *whose voice is this, actually?* is how you begin to tell your own conscience apart from the one that was put there to keep you in line.

There's a simple test that helped Renee, and it may help you. When the guilt speaks, listen for the *pronouns and the tone*. Your own conscience, when you've genuinely done wrong, tends to be specific and oddly calm: *that was unkind, you should apologize for what you said.* It points at an action and offers a repair. The installed voice is different — it's global, contemptuous, and total: *you're selfish, you're a disappointment, you ruin everything, this is who you are.* One is correction; the other is contempt, the very contempt we named in the first chapter, now coming from inside your own head in someone else's accent. Renee started catching it in the act. She'd feel the wave of *how could you be so cold* and stop to ask whether those were words she would ever, in a thousand years, say to a friend in her situation. They weren't. They were her mother's words, memorized so young she'd mistaken them for her own. Naming the voice doesn't silence it immediately, but it strips it of authority, the way a threat loses its power the moment you recognize the bluff behind it.

And here is the distinction that will do more work than any other: the difference between guilt and grief. They feel similar from the inside — both heavy, both aching — so people confuse them constantly, and the confusion is expensive. Guilt says *I did something wrong.* Grief says *this just hurts.* They call for completely different responses. If you've genuinely violated your own values — and I want to be honest that this is possible, because not all guilt is false and a mature person doesn't dismiss every pang as "toxic" — then real guilt is a good teacher, and the answer is to make it right. But most of what people feel after stepping back from a toxic relationship is not guilt at all. It's grief. It doesn't hurt because you did something wrong; it hurts because you lost something, or never had it, or had to give up the hope of it. Renee's tide was grief wearing guilt's clothing. When she finally asked, honestly, *did I actually do something wrong, or does this just hurt?*, the answer was almost always the second — and grief, unlike guilt, is not corrected by going back. It's carried, and slowly set down.

Choosing yourself is not the same as abandoning them, no matter how identical the two can feel. Abandonment is walking away from someone who depends on you and whom you're genuinely obligated to, out of selfishness or cruelty. What you're doing is different in kind: you are declining to keep sacrificing yourself to someone who has used your loyalty against you. The toxic dynamic works hard to blur that line, because if it can convince you that any self-protection equals abandonment, it can make your very survival feel like a sin. But a grown child stepping back from a harmful parent has not "abandoned" them; the parent remains an adult, responsible for their own life, with their own choices about whether to change. Renee did not abandon her mother — she still called, still saw her, still cared. She simply stopped setting herself on fire to keep the woman warm. Even Daniel, who cut off contact entirely, did not abandon his father in any moral sense; he protected himself and his children from a man who had chosen, again and again, not to be safe. Refusing to be destroyed is not the same as abandoning someone. It only feels that way because you were taught to measure your goodness by how much of yourself you'd surrender.

Making Peace With Your Choice

You are allowed to wish them well and still stay far away. People imagine there are only two positions — loving closeness or bitter cutoff — and so they assume that if you've created distance, you must hate the person, and that if you *don't* hate them, you're obligated to go back. Neither is true. You can hold genuine goodwill for someone, hope their life goes gently, even love them in a real if complicated way, and still know that being near them costs you more than you can pay. Renee landed exactly there with her mother: not hatred, not estrangement, but a warm, watchful distance. Daniel landed there too, in his own way — no contact, and yet, when he spoke of his father, no venom either, just a quiet wish that the man might somehow find peace, at a safe remove from Daniel's life. Wishing someone well from a distance is not a contradiction. It is often the most honest and durable form love can take when closeness has proven unsafe.

When the "how could you" comes — and it will, from others and from your own 3 a.m. mind — you'll want a true answer ready. The people asking it are often certain and loud, and the version of the question that comes from inside you, in the dark, is worse. You do not owe the loud outside version a defense; "this was the healthiest thing I could do, and I've made my peace with it" is a complete answer, and you're not required to litigate your childhood to satisfy a cousin's curiosity. But the inside version deserves a real reply, and here it is, the one to keep: *I did not do this lightly, I tried the things worth trying, and I chose to stop being harmed. That is allowed.* Say it as many times as the night requires. Guilt manufactured to control you thrives on the sense that you owe everyone an explanation and have never quite given a good enough one. The freedom is in realizing the case was closed a long time ago, and you were the only judge who ever actually had standing.

Daniel faced the loud version directly at a family funeral, where a relative cornered him and demanded, in front of others, how he could have "done that to his own father." He told me later that the old panic rose up — the urge to explain, to produce the hospital records, to make the relative understand. And then something settled in him, and he simply said, "I made the right decision for me and my kids. I'm at peace with it." He didn't raise his voice. He didn't defend. He repeated a version of it once more when pressed, and then he changed the subject and walked away. The relative was unsatisfied, of course; people invested in the old story usually are. But Daniel discovered what most people in his shoes eventually do: you cannot be argued out of a peace you've genuinely made, and the refusal to defend is itself the strongest possible statement that the matter is settled. The ones who demand you re-litigate your choice are rarely seeking to understand. They're seeking to reopen a case you've earned the right to keep closed.

Finally, the quietest and most radical permission of all: you're allowed to have simply needed to leave. So much of the guilt insists that your reasons weren't severe enough — that unless there was violence, unless you can produce a catalog of unforgivable acts, you had no right to step back, and stepping back over "just" chronic disrespect or coldness or being worn down makes you dramatic and ungrateful. Let that go. You do not need to prove your suffering reached some official threshold to have been allowed to protect yourself.

"It was slowly destroying me, and I needed it to stop" is reason enough. You don't have to hate them, don't have to have a tidy story the whole family accepts, don't have to wait for anyone's permission or agreement — we settled that back in Part One. You only had to need it. That was always enough. In the next chapter, we turn to the thing that ambushes almost everyone who makes it this far: not the guilt of leaving, but the strange, powerful pull to go *back* — and why missing someone who hurt you is not the sign you fear it is.

Chapter Eight — The Pull Back In

Six weeks into the calmest stretch of her adult life, Renee found herself with her thumb hovering over her mother's number, seized by a longing so sudden and so physical it frightened her. Nothing had happened. No crisis, no invitation. She had simply been folding laundry on a quiet Sunday when a wave of missing rolled through her — missing her mother, of all people, missing her so acutely that the distance she'd fought so hard to build suddenly felt like a cruel mistake she needed to undo right now, tonight, before it was too late. If this has happened to you — if you've done the brave work of getting free and then found yourself aching to go straight back — I need you to hear the first and most important thing in this chapter: that pull is not a sign that you were wrong. It is the most predictable thing in the world, it has a mechanism, and it passes. Let's take it apart, so the next time it comes you'll recognize it instead of obeying it.

The Machinery of the Pull

First, the pull is often manufactured from the outside, through a maneuver called hoovering. Named for the vacuum, it's the toxic person's move to suck you back in the moment they sense you slipping away for real. It rarely looks like an apology, because a genuine apology isn't the goal — reeling you back is. Instead it arrives as sudden, dazzling warmth: the loving message out of nowhere, the "I was just thinking about you," the birthday card that's kinder than any word they said all year. Or it comes as a crisis — an illness, an emergency, a sudden vulnerability that only you can answer, because they know your compassion is the one door that never fully locks. Renee's mother was a master of the timed thaw; every time Renee's distance became genuine rather than reactive, a warm little message would appear, precisely calibrated to reopen the wound of hope. Recognizing hoovering for what it is — a technique, not a transformation — takes away most of its power. The test is simple: is this a real, sustained change backed by different behavior over time, or is it a burst of exactly the warmth you're most starved for, arriving right when you were finally getting free?

Second, even without their help, your own memory conspires against you, because the good memories shout while the bad ones go quiet. This isn't a personal failing; it's how memory works for almost everyone. Psychologists call it rosy retrospection — the mind's tendency to soften the sharp edges of the past and let the warm moments glow. In an ordinary relationship this is a harmless mercy. In a toxic one it's a trap, because the very pain that drove you out begins to blur and fade, while the rare good afternoons remain vivid and beckoning. Weeks after leaving, you'll find yourself replaying the tender moments in high definition and struggling to summon the daily dread that was your actual life. The relationship you miss is a highlight reel, edited by your own protective brain, and it bears very little resemblance to the full, unedited footage you were living in a few short weeks ago.

And third, underneath both of these runs the deepest current: the chemistry of it is closer to addiction than most people are comfortable admitting. We built the foundation for this back in Part One — the intermittent, unpredictable reward that forges a fierce and desperate bond. Here's why the pull to return feels so much like a craving: because chemically, it more or less is one. The same neural machinery that makes a substance hard to quit is engaged by a person who dispensed love on an unpredictable schedule. That's why leaving can produce something very like withdrawal — the restlessness, the obsessive thoughts, the physical ache, the 3 a.m. certainty that one more hit of contact would make it all stop. Understanding this reframes the entire experience. You are not weak-willed, and you are not still in love against your own better judgment. You are a person going through withdrawal from a bond that was engineered, whether the other person understood what they were doing or not, to be chemically hard to leave. Withdrawal is brutal, and withdrawal ends. Both are true.

Priya felt this in her body more than her mind. In the first month after leaving Dev, she would find herself, at odd hours, physically reaching for her phone to text him — not out of any conscious decision, but the way a smoker's hand drifts to a shirt pocket that no longer holds a pack. The absence of him was a presence, a low static that filled her apartment. She told a friend, ashamed, that she must still love him, because how else could leaving a man who treated her so badly hurt this much? Her friend, who had been through it herself, said something Priya never forgot: "You don't miss him. You're in withdrawal from him. Give it time and see what's actually left when the drug wears off." What was left, months later, was not love. It was relief, and a slowly dawning astonishment that she had lived that way for so long. But she had to get through the withdrawal to find out — and in the thick of it, the ache had disguised itself, convincingly, as love.

The Longing That Isn't What It Seems

When you examine the longing honestly, you usually find you're missing the hope, not the person. This is one of the most freeing distinctions in the whole book, so sit with it. What Renee ached for that Sunday, when she looked closely, was not actually her mother as her mother truly was — the criticism, the cold weeks, the exhausting management of it all. What she ached for was the mother she'd always hoped to have, the warm and safe one she'd caught glimpses of and spent her whole life trying to make permanent. That woman was a fantasy, assembled from the good afternoons and the desperate wishing. And you cannot go back to a fantasy, because it was never there to return to. The person you'd actually be returning to is the real one, with the real behavior, on repeat. Naming the longing precisely — *I miss the hope of who they could have been, not the reality of who they were* — drains it of its false urgency, because you realize the thing you're reaching for was never on offer in the first place.

The pull is also strongest exactly when you're most depleted, which is why it so often

comes at 3 a.m. Loneliness, exhaustion, a hard day, a glass of wine, the particular ache of a holiday — these are the conditions under which the doubt creeps in and whispers its favorite question: *was it really even that bad?* Notice that the question never arrives when you're rested, busy, and surrounded by people who love you. It waits for the low moments, because it needs your defenses down to be persuasive. Renee learned to distrust any reconsideration of her whole life that arrived at three in the morning on a lonely night. The insight you have at your lowest is not wiser than the one you reached in daylight, with a clear head, after months of evidence. It only feels more urgent. When the "was it that bad" question comes in the dark, the answer is not to answer it then. It's to notice the *conditions* it chose to arrive in, and to wait for morning before you trust anything it says.

There's a useful rule people in recovery from all sorts of things swear by, and it fits here perfectly: never make a decision about the relationship when you are Hungry, Angry, Lonely, or Tired. Those four states — easy to remember by their first letters — are precisely when your judgment is compromised and the pull is strongest, and they are almost always the states you're in when the urge to reach out ambushes you. Renee added a small practice to this: when the doubt came at night, she would name the condition out loud. *I'm not reconsidering my whole life. I'm lonely and it's late.* Naming it shrank it back to its true size. The thought that felt like a profound reckoning revealed itself as a tired, lonely person at midnight — which is not a reliable narrator, and never was.

The most useful skill here is learning to fact-check your own softening memory in real time. When the rosy reel starts playing, don't argue with the feeling — interrogate the footage. Pick the warm memory your mind is offering and ask what happened *right before* it, and right after. That perfect holiday: how did it actually end? That tender phone call: what was the cost of the week around it? Renee would catch herself glowing over some rare kindness of her mother's and deliberately follow the thread forward to what always came next — the little dig, the cold turn, the price. I want to be honest that this cuts both ways: the goal is not to build the ugliest possible case against them, because that's just distortion in the other direction, and you deserve the truth more than you deserve a verdict. The goal is *accuracy* — to replace the edited highlight reel with the full, honest footage, good moments and all, so you're deciding based on what the relationship actually was rather than on the fantasy your lonely brain is selling you at midnight.

Staying Gone

This is where that mental list finally becomes a tool instead of a torment. For most of her life, Renee kept a running tally in her head that talked her *out* of her own experience — *that wasn't so bad, you're overreacting*. Now she built the opposite list, and this time she wrote it down. On a note in her phone she kept a plain, unsentimental record: the specific things that had actually happened, in her own words, written on days when she saw clearly. Not a hate list — an honesty list, a piece of testimony from her clear-eyed self to her weak-moment self.

Because the cruelest thing about the pull is that it arrives precisely when your memory is least reliable, and a person in withdrawal cannot always be trusted to recall why they quit. So you leave yourself a message from higher ground. When the 3 a.m. longing comes and the reel starts to glow, you don't have to win the argument in your head. You just have to open the note and read what you already know to be true.

And when the craving itself comes, the skill is to ride it without acting on it, because a craving is a wave, not a permanent state. People assume an urge will only build and build until they give in, so they give in to make it stop. But that's not how urges actually behave. Left unanswered, a craving rises, crests, and falls — usually within twenty or thirty minutes, sometimes less. If you can put even a little time and friction between the impulse and the action — call a friend, go for a walk, open your honesty list, simply promise yourself you'll wait an hour before you do anything — you'll very often find the wave has passed on its own, and the certainty that felt so overwhelming has quietly dissolved. Renee's rule became simple: *I don't have to never call her again. I just have to not call her tonight.* That was always doable, and "tonight" kept turning into another week, and another.

Here is the promise that makes all of it worth it: every single time you don't go back, the pull loses a little of its grip. This is the flip side of the addiction — the same machinery that made the bond strong will, in reverse, let it weaken, if you stop feeding it. Each craving you ride out without giving in teaches your nervous system that the wave passes and you survive. Each hoover you recognize and decline chips away at the reflex. The longing that felt unbearable in week six becomes a dull ache in month three and a passing thought by month nine — not because you forced yourself to stop caring, but because you stopped renewing the bond, and bonds that aren't renewed slowly fade. That Sunday, Renee put the phone down, folded the rest of the laundry, and called a friend instead. The wave passed, as it always did. And she was still gone in the morning, and a little more free than she'd been the night before. In the next chapter, we'll turn to the grief that lives underneath all this longing — because much of what pulls you back is really something asking to be mourned, and mourning, not returning, is what finally sets it down.

Chapter Nine — Grieving Who They Never Were

Renee expected to feel free. She had done everything right — seen it clearly, set the boundaries, created the distance, made her peace with the guilt, learned to ride out the pull. And underneath the freedom, to her confusion, was something that felt a great deal like mourning, as if someone had died. *Why am I grieving?* she asked, almost angry at herself. *She's not even dead. And she hurt me. What is there to grieve?* If you've asked that question, this chapter is the answer, and it's the last stop in Part Two, because grief turns out to be the hidden work underneath all the breaking free. Much of what pulls you back is really something asking to be mourned. And grief, unlike returning, is what actually lets you set it down.

The Real Loss

You are grieving the relationship you needed and never actually got. This is the first thing to understand, because it dissolves the confusion of mourning someone who hurt you. You're not grieving the cruelty. You're grieving its absence — the mother who never showed up, the partner who never became safe, the friend who was never truly on your side. Renee wasn't mourning the woman who criticized and withdrew and rewrote the past. She was mourning the mother she'd needed her whole life and never had: the one who'd have been proud without competing, warm without conditions, safe to come home to. That mother was real as a need and never real as a person, and her absence is a genuine loss, maybe the largest one there is. You can grieve something you never had. In fact that is often the deepest grief of all, because there's no memory of it to comfort you — only the shape of the hole where it should have been.

It's a double grief, and naming both halves matters. You're losing them — the actual person, whatever they were — and at the same time you're losing the hope of them, the future in which they finally became who you needed. That second loss is often the heavier one, and it's the one people miss. For years the hope had been load-bearing; it was the thing that kept you trying, the "next time it'll be different" that organized your whole relationship with them. Giving up the relationship means giving up that hope, and the hope had become so much a part of you that its death feels like losing a limb. Renee could survive losing the closeness she'd had. What nearly undid her was losing the closeness she'd always believed was still coming — the reconciliation scene she'd played in her head a thousand times, the someday when her mother would finally see her. Grieving means letting that someday die. It was never going to arrive, but you still have to bury it.

Renee could describe the fantasy in detail, because she'd rehearsed it for most of her life. In it, her mother grew old and soft, and one afternoon simply understood — took Renee's hands and said she was sorry, that she saw now what she'd done, that Renee had always been enough. In the fantasy Renee wept and forgave and they had whatever years were left as the mother and daughter they were always meant to be. It was a beautiful scene, and letting go of it felt like a betrayal, as though giving up the fantasy meant giving up on her mother. But it wasn't her mother she was releasing. It was the script — the private, cherished movie in which everything was finally made right. Grieving, for Renee, meant admitting that the reconciliation scene belonged to a woman who did not exist, and mourning it the way you'd mourn any beloved thing that was never coming. Some of the heaviest grief there is attaches to scenes that never happened and now never will.

And it's a strange kind of grief, because the person is usually still alive — what's called ambiguous loss. Ordinary grief has a body, a funeral, a casserole brigade, a clear before and after. This has none of that. The person you're mourning is still out there, still posting photos, still being spoken of at holidays, sometimes still in your life in a reduced form. There's no funeral for a mother who's alive and shopping across town, no ritual for the end of a relationship that technically still exists. This ambiguity makes the grief harder to feel and far harder to have witnessed, because the world doesn't recognize it as loss at all. You're mourning, and everyone around you thinks nothing has died. That loneliness — grieving a loss no one else can see — is one of the heaviest parts, and simply having a name for it, *ambiguous loss*, can make it feel less like you're losing your mind and more like you're facing something real that many others have faced too.

Letting the Grief Be Complicated

You will feel anger and love in the same breath, and both are allowed to be true. People expect grief to be pure — pure sorrow, or pure relief — and this grief is anything but. One hour you'll ache with love and miss them terribly; the next you'll be furious at what they did, and then ashamed of the fury, and then aching again. This is not confusion or instability. It's the honest complexity of mourning a person who was neither all bad nor all good, who genuinely loved you in their broken way and genuinely harmed you in the same breath. If you try to resolve the contradiction — to decide they were purely a villain so you're allowed to be angry, or purely a victim so you're allowed to love them — you'll do violence to the truth and stall the grief. Let both live. You can hate what someone did and miss them at the same time. Renee learned to stop policing which feeling was "correct" and let them come as they came, and only then did they start to move.

You're also grieving more than the person — you're grieving the years, and the version of yourself that kept waiting. This is a loss people rarely give themselves permission to mourn, and it deserves it. There's the childhood you didn't get, if this began there — the safety and delight that should have been your birthright and weren't. There are the years, sometimes decades, spent managing and hoping and shrinking. And there's a particular figure to mourn: the version of you who kept waiting, who kept believing, who kept pouring herself into a relationship that couldn't hold her. Renee grieved the little girl rehearsing apologies in the hallway, and she also grieved the grown woman who'd spent her thirties still auditioning for her mother's approval. Mourning that waiting self is not self-pity. It's honoring the real cost of what happened, and it's a necessary goodbye — because you can't fully step into who you're becoming while still unconsciously mourning who you had to be.

And you will feel relief and guilt at the very same moment — free and sad at once. There's a specific, disorienting experience that catches people off guard: the wave of relief that comes with distance, immediately chased by guilt for feeling relieved. *What kind of person is relieved to lose their own mother?* The answer is: a person who was carrying something heavy for a very long time and has finally set part of it down. Relief is not proof of coldness; it's proof of how much the relationship cost you, and it can coexist perfectly with real sorrow. You can feel lighter and heartbroken in the same afternoon. Renee described the strangeness of crying in her car one day, unable to tell whether the tears were grief or relief, and slowly understanding they were both, braided together so tightly they'd become a single feeling. That braid is not a sign something's wrong with you. It's simply what freedom feels like when it arrives with a loss attached.

Moving Through It

Grief has to be felt to move — grief avoided is grief prolonged. This is the hard, unglamorous heart of it, and it runs against every instinct to stay busy, stay strong, and get over it. But grief is not a problem to be solved or a mood to be managed around; it's an experience that has to be moved *through*, and the only way through is to actually feel it. The tears you swallow, the sorrow you outrun, the anger you deny — none of it disappears. It goes underground and waits, leaking out as depression, or numbness, or that inexplicable pull to go back. Renee's Sunday longing, it turned out, was largely grief she hadn't let herself feel, showing up in disguise. When she finally sat down and let the sadness come — actually cried, actually raged, actually let herself miss what she'd never had — it began, at last, to loosen. Feeling it is not wallowing. Wallowing is grief that circles without moving; true grieving moves, even when it's slow, even when it doesn't feel like progress. You have to let it in for it to ever leave.

Because there's no funeral, you may have to make your own rituals of goodbye. Grief has always used ritual to move — the service, the burial, the sitting together — and this loss offers none of them by default, so it helps to build your own. People do this in countless ways: writing the letter you'll never send and then burning it, or keeping it; marking a private date as the end of the waiting; giving away an object that held the old hope; saying the goodbye aloud to an empty room; visiting a place that meant something and leaving it there. The point isn't the specific act. It's giving the grief a container and a moment — a way to mark that something has ended, since the world won't mark it for you. Renee wrote her mother a long letter she never mailed, saying everything she'd never say in person, and then folded it into a box she rarely opened. It changed nothing between her and her mother. It changed something in *her,* which was the entire point.

Priya's ritual was smaller and more physical. Months after the divorce, she finally took down the last photograph of her wedding day that had lingered, half-forgotten, on a shelf. She'd kept it not out of love but out of a vague sense that removing it would be admitting something. When she finally wrapped it and put it away, she was surprised to find herself crying — not for Dev, but for the young woman in the white dress who had believed, on that day, that she was beginning a good life. She said goodbye to that hopeful bride out loud, alone in her apartment, and something in her chest that had been clenched for years quietly let go. These rituals sound almost too simple to matter. They matter enormously. Grief is not moved by insight alone; it is moved by *doing* something that tells the deepest part of you the truth — that this has ended, that it is time to lay it down.

And the closure you've been waiting for — you're going to have to give it to yourself, because they were never going to hand it to you. This is perhaps the final, liberating truth of Part Two. We wait, sometimes for years, for the apology that would let us move on: the moment they finally understand, admit it, say they're sorry, release us. For most people reading this, that moment is not coming. The person who harmed you is behind their own wall, in their own story, and waiting for them to walk through it and grant you peace is waiting for a gift they do not have to give. So you stop waiting. You give yourself the closure instead — not by pretending it didn't happen, but by deciding that your healing no longer requires their participation. Closure was never really a thing they could hand you anyway; it was always something you build, on your own side of the wall, out of acceptance and grief and time. Renee stopped waiting for her mother to understand, and in that surrender found the freedom she'd been trying to extract from her mother for thirty years. That is where Part Two ends: not with them changed, but with you released. You've seen it, left it, and grieved it. What remains is the best part, and the hardest — building a life that is finally, fully your own. That is Part Three, and it begins now.

PART THREE

Rebuilding

Chapter Ten — Learning to Trust Yourself Again

The distance held. The grief moved. And Renee, finally standing in the quiet life she'd fought so hard to build, discovered a problem she hadn't expected: she no longer trusted herself to run it. Small decisions paralyzed her. She'd second-guess which restaurant to pick, then second-guess the second-guessing. When something felt wrong, she'd immediately talk herself out of the feeling, because feeling things wrongly was the crime she'd been convicted of her whole life. She had spent decades being told her perceptions were faulty, her reactions excessive, her memory unreliable — and now that no one was saying it anymore, she said it to herself. Getting free of the person, she learned, is not the same as getting free of what they installed. This chapter, the first of Part Three, is about the most important repair of all: learning to trust your own mind again, because every other thing you rebuild will stand on that foundation.

The Self-Doubt They Left Behind

Gaslighting doesn't just win arguments; it hollows out your inner compass. When someone spends years telling you that you didn't see what you saw and didn't feel what you felt, they're not merely being difficult in the moment — they're slowly dismantling the instrument you use to navigate reality. A compass works only if you trust the needle. Renee's needle still worked; it still swung toward *this is wrong, this hurts, this isn't* *right.* But she'd been trained to distrust it so completely that every time it moved, she overrode it, assuming the error was hers. That's the deep damage of gaslighting: not that it makes you wrong, but that it severs your confidence in being right, so that even a working compass becomes useless because you no longer believe what it tells you. The needle was never actually broken. The trust in it was, and that is what you're here to rebuild.

The result is a mind that second-guesses everything, the long echo of years spent walking on eggshells. When you've lived in an environment where any read could be "wrong" and punished, your mind learns to check itself compulsively, running every perception past an imagined judge before daring to act on it. Long after the judge is gone, the habit runs on. You'll form an opinion and immediately hunt for why it's unfair. You'll feel a clear preference and then dismiss it as selfish. You'll sense that someone's treating you badly and instantly generate five excuses for them. This isn't indecision as a personality trait; it's a trained response, the mental equivalent of flinching, installed by an environment where trusting yourself was dangerous. Naming it as an echo rather than a fact about who you are is the first step, because an echo, unlike a wall, eventually fades when the sound that caused it stops.

Renee noticed how far it had spread when a coworker was short with her one morning, and she spent the entire day constructing an elaborate case for how she must have done something to deserve it — replaying the week, hunting for her crime — before it even occurred to her that the coworker might simply have been having a bad day that had nothing to do with her. That was the reflex in miniature: her mind's automatic assumption that any friction must be her fault, any coldness a punishment she'd earned. In a healthy life, most of what other people do is about them, not you. But a mind trained in a toxic environment reflexively takes responsibility for everyone's moods, because that hypervigilant self-blame was once the only way to feel any control. Catching the reflex — *wait, this might not be about me at all* — was, for Renee, like discovering a thief who'd been quietly emptying her pockets for years.

And you'll notice you still brace for a blow that isn't coming anymore. This is one of the strangest and most telling aftereffects. You're safe now, and yet your body keeps preparing for impact — the flinch when a partner raises their voice even slightly, the spike of dread when a text arrives, the reflexive apology when nothing's wrong, the way you still scan a happy room for the mood that's about to turn. Your nervous system learned, at great effort, that vigilance kept you safe, and it doesn't update just because your circumstances did. This can be discouraging — *shouldn't I be over this by now?* — but it's not a sign of failure or of damage that won't heal. It's a sign that your alarm system worked exactly as designed and simply hasn't yet received the news that the threat is gone. Part of rebuilding is gently, repeatedly, teaching it the news: *that was then. I'm safe now. I can put the shield down.*

Rebuilding the Inner Compass

You rebuild self-trust the way you rebuild anyone's trust: through small promises kept. You would not trust a person who constantly broke their word to you, and the same is true of your relationship with yourself. If you're forever promising to rest and then overriding it, to say no and then caving, to start the thing and then abandoning it, some part of you quietly concludes that you are not reliable — and self-trust erodes. The repair is almost embarrassingly small at first, and that's exactly why it works. You make a tiny promise to yourself and you keep it. *I'll take the walk. I'll go to bed at eleven. I'll speak up in that meeting.* Each kept promise is a deposit in an account that toxic years overdrew, a small piece of evidence that you can rely on yourself. Renee started with something almost laughably minor — a promise to drink her coffee in silence each morning without checking her phone — and kept it, day after day, and was surprised how much steadier she felt. Self-trust isn't restored by a grand act of courage. It's restored by a thousand small acts of follow-through, until you become, in your own eyes, a person whose word means something.

You also have to relearn your own yes and your own no — to reconnect with the gut they trained you to ignore. For years, your instincts were overruled, so you stopped consulting them; it hurt less not to want things you weren't allowed to have. Now you get to reawaken them, and it starts with the smallest, lowest-stakes questions. What do *you* actually want for dinner? Which of these do *you* prefer, before considering what anyone else thinks?

Do you actually want to go to this, or are you going out of obligation? These questions feel trivial and are anything but, because each one reconnects a wire that was cut. Renee realized she genuinely did not know her own favorite things anymore — she'd spent so long organizing around her mother's preferences that her own had gone silent. Rebuilding meant asking, over and over, in matters small enough to be safe: *what do I want here?* — and then honoring the answer, so her gut learned that speaking up would no longer get it punished.

And you have to relearn that your feelings are information, not overreactions to be managed away. You were taught that your emotions were the problem — too much, too sensitive, always wrong — so you learned to treat every feeling as a symptom to suppress. But feelings are data. Anger often signals a boundary has been crossed; unease frequently registers something not yet consciously named; the flat dread around a certain person is worth heeding. Now, I'll keep faith with what we said all the way back in the first chapter: feelings are evidence, not verdicts. The goal is not to swing to the other extreme and treat every emotion as infallible truth that must be obeyed — that's its own kind of trap. The goal is to *listen* to your feelings again, to take them seriously as information, and then to weigh them with a clear head. A feeling is a message worth reading. You just get to be the one who decides what to do about it — which is a role you were never allowed before.

Becoming Your Own Safe Person

The critical inner voice they left behind can be replaced — slowly — by a kinder one. Most people coming out of a toxic relationship carry an inner narrator that sounds a lot like their tormentor: harsh, contemptuous, quick to call them stupid, selfish, or too much. You can't simply delete that voice, but you can build a second one alongside it and practice choosing it, until it grows louder than the old one. Here's the key, and it draws the whole book together: the kind voice is not a flatterer who tells you you're perfect. That would be as false as the cruel one. The healthy inner voice is a good *corrector* — the difference we named in the very first chapter. When you fall short, it says, like a person who loves you would, *that wasn't your best, and you can make it right,* instead of *you're worthless, you always ruin everything*. It can hold you accountable without holding you in contempt. Learning to talk to yourself the way a good, honest friend would — warm and truthful at once — is not softness. It's the most practical skill in this chapter, because that voice is the one you'll live inside for the rest of your life.

A practice that helps: when you catch the cruel voice mid-sentence, try asking whether you would say those exact words to someone you loved who'd made the same mistake. Renee tried this after a genuine misstep at work — she'd dropped a ball, and the old voice was already calling her a fraud who'd finally been exposed. She stopped and asked what she'd say to a friend in the same spot. The answer came easily: *you're human, you were stretched thin, fix what you can and let the rest go.* The gap between the two voices stunned her. She would never have spoken to a friend, or even a stranger, with the contempt she reserved for herself. That gap is where the work lives. You are not trying to excuse your mistakes; you're trying to meet them with the same fair, honest kindness you'd offer anyone else — the correction a decent person gives, not the contempt a cruel one does. Over time, extending yourself that ordinary courtesy stops feeling indulgent and starts feeling like simple justice.

Self-trust is the foundation everything else gets built on, which is why it comes first in Part Three. Notice how much of what's ahead depends on it. You can't set a boundary you don't trust yourself to keep. You can't leave a bad situation next time if you don't trust your own read that it's bad. You can't let a good person in if you can't trust your own judgment about who's safe. Every other repair in this final part — rediscovering who you are, letting the good ones in — rests on this one. That's why we don't rush past it. When you can once again trust your own perceptions, keep your own promises, and speak to yourself with honest kindness, you've rebuilt the platform that the rest of your life stands on. Everything else is construction; this is the foundation.

And in the end, this is the birthright being restored to you: you are allowed to be the authority on your own life. For years, someone else was the final word — on what happened, on what you felt, on what you were worth, on what you were allowed to want. Reclaiming self-trust means quietly taking that authority back and refusing to hand it out again. It doesn't mean you stop listening to others or think you're never wrong; the authority on your own life still seeks counsel, still admits mistakes, still grows. It simply means the final say about your experience, your choices, and your worth returns to its rightful owner — you. Renee marked the shift the day she caught herself about to text a friend to ask whether she was "overreacting" to something, and instead paused and decided she trusted her own read. It was a small moment. It was also the whole thing. In the next chapter, we'll build on this foundation and turn to a question self-trust finally makes it safe to ask: underneath all the roles you had to play to survive them, who are you actually — and who do you want to become?

Chapter Eleven — Who You Are Without Them

Once Renee could trust herself again, a stranger question surfaced, quieter than all the others and somehow more unsettling: *who am I, exactly?* She had spent so long being someone's daughter-shaped solution — the fixer, the one who managed, the one who absorbed — that when the managing stopped, she found a kind of blank where a self should be. She knew what she was against now. She was less sure what she was *for*. If you've felt that disorientation, that hollow just past the freedom, I want to reassure you at the outset: the self you're looking for is not gone. It went quiet to survive, which is a very different thing from gone. This chapter is about coaxing it back out — and then, better than recovery, about getting to decide who you become from here.

The Self That Got Buried

Parts of you went quiet in order to survive, and that silence was intelligent, not weak. In a toxic environment, certain traits are dangerous to have out in the open. If your honesty got punished, honesty learned to hide. If your joy invited resentment or competition, you learned to dim it. If your needs were treated as burdens, you stopped having them, at least where anyone could see. This wasn't you losing yourself through carelessness; it was a survival strategy, and a shrewd one. You buried the parts that drew fire, exactly as a soldier keeps his head down. The problem is that the burying becomes automatic and outlasts the war, so that long after the danger passes, whole regions of you remain underground out of a caution no longer needed. Recovery starts with respecting why they hid before you go looking for them. They didn't abandon you. You sent them into hiding to keep them safe, and now you get to tell them it's over.

You are more than the role you were cast in — you are not the fixer, the scapegoat, or the peacekeeper. We met these roles back in Part One, and here is where you finally step out of them. The trouble is that a role played long enough stops feeling like a costume and starts feeling like your skin. Renee genuinely believed she *was* "the responsible one who holds everyone together" — not that she'd been assigned that job, but that it was her very nature. Untangling self from role means asking a disorienting question: if I weren't the fixer, who would I be? It can feel like standing at the edge of a void, because the role was load-bearing; it told you what to do in every room. But the void is not emptiness. It's space — the room a self needs to exist in. You are not the function you performed for other people. You are the person underneath it, who was always more than the job.

There's a particular grief and freedom in realizing how much of your "personality" was actually a survival adaptation. The people-pleaser discovers that their endless accommodation wasn't generosity but fear wearing generosity's face. The hyper-competent one realizes their compulsive reliability was a bid for a safety that never came. This can be disorienting — *if that wasn't really me, what is?* — but it's also enormously hopeful, because it means you're not stuck with traits you never chose. Renee had always thought of herself as "just a naturally anxious person." It took stepping out of the role to see that the anxiety wasn't her nature; it was the residue of a job she'd been drafted into as a child. Freed from the job, she was startled to meet a version of herself that was, underneath it all, fairly calm. She hadn't known that person existed. She'd been too busy holding everyone together to ever meet her.

And somewhere along the way, you quietly set down your own tastes, opinions, and dreams. This is the subtlest theft. It rarely happens in one dramatic surrender; it happens through a thousand small abdications, each too minor to notice. Your opinion got overruled so often you stopped forming one. Your preferences were inconvenient, so you defaulted to theirs. The dream you mentioned once was met with a laugh or a lecture, so you folded it away and stopped mentioning it. Renee realized, with a jolt, that she couldn't reliably name her favorite music, her own politics, or what she'd do with a free Saturday, because for decades those questions had been answered by someone else's preferences and moods. This is not the same as having no self. It's having a self that was systematically talked out of taking up space. And what was set down can be picked back up, which is exactly what the middle of this chapter is for.

Rediscovering You

You find yourself again through small experiments — low-stakes tries at your own preferences. You don't recover a self by staring inward and demanding it announce itself; you recover it by *doing*, in small, safe ways, and noticing what feels alive. Try the cuisine you never got to choose. Read the book, see the film, take the class, wear the color. Treat it like gentle research rather than a test you can fail: not "I must discover my one true passion," just "let me see what I'm drawn to when no one's judging." Some experiments will fall flat, and that's information too. Renee started absurdly small — she bought flowers she liked for a table no one inspected, cooked a dish her mother would have criticized, spent a Saturday exactly as she pleased and reported to no one. Each small choice, made purely on her own preference, was a vote for a self she was slowly electing back into being. The self is not found in one revelation. It's assembled from many small, honest choices about what you actually like.

You also rebuild the outer things — a routine, a space, a life that belong to you. The inner recovery wants an outer home. Look at your days and your rooms and ask what's there out of old obligation versus genuine choice. Rearrange the space so it reflects you, not the ghost of someone's disapproval. Build a morning that's yours, keep the traditions that mean something and quietly drop the ones you only ever performed for others. This is not superficial; our environments and rhythms shape us, and for years yours were shaped around managing someone else. Renee repainted a room her mother had once declared the wrong color, and every time she walked past it she felt, in a small concrete way, that this life was finally hers to author. Reclaiming the outer scaffolding of your life gives the recovering self a place to actually live.

And you need new witnesses — people who reflect the real you back to you. Recall how isolation shrank your world and left the toxic person as your only mirror, showing you a distorted, unflattering reflection you slowly mistook for the truth. Part of becoming yourself is deliberately gathering better mirrors: people who see you clearly and like what they see, who reflect back your humor and your worth and your goodness. We become ourselves partly through the eyes of others, which is precisely why the toxic person's distorted gaze was so damaging — and why steady, kind witnesses are so healing. Renee noticed she felt more herself around a particular friend, freer, funnier, more solid, and she began, on purpose, to spend more time with the people in whose company she liked who she was. Choose your mirrors carefully now. You've spent long enough seeing yourself in a cracked one.

Reclaiming Your Story

The deepest shift is going from a character in their story to the author of your own. For years you had a part written for you — the difficult one, the ungrateful one, the one who was lucky anyone put up with her. Reclaiming yourself means picking up the pen. You are no longer a supporting character in someone else's drama, defined by the role they cast; you are the author of your own life, and you decide what it's about now. This is not about denying what happened. It's about who holds the pen going forward — whether your life is still organized around them, even in opposition, or whether it becomes genuinely *yours*, pointed at what you care about rather than at them at all. Renee spent the first stretch of freedom still defining herself against her mother. The real turn came when she stopped writing a story about escaping her mother and started writing one that was simply about her own life, in which her mother was, at last, a minor character.

Part of authoring your story is making meaning of it — but without forced silver linings or toxic positivity. There's enormous pressure to tie suffering up in a bow: *everything happens for a reason, it made me stronger, I wouldn't change a thing.* I want to give you full permission to reject all of that. You are not required to be grateful for what happened, and it's both truer and healthier to say *that should not have happened to me, and I have built something meaningful anyway.* Real meaning-making isn't pretending the wound was a gift. It's deciding what you'll do with the fact of it — the compassion it gave you, the clarity you earned, the way you'll refuse to pass the pattern on. Renee never reached "I'm grateful for it," and she didn't need to. She reached something sturdier: *it was wrong, and I'm proud of who I became in spite of it.* That is meaning without denial, and it holds weight that a forced silver lining never could.

I want to guard you against a specific pressure here, because well-meaning people will apply it: the pressure to declare yourself healed, grateful, and wiser, tied up neatly for their comfort. Some of that pressure even comes dressed as spirituality — *forgive and be grateful, it was all part of your growth.* You are allowed to decline. You can acknowledge that hard things sometimes forge real strengths without ever endorsing the idea that the harm was therefore good, or necessary, or a gift in disguise. A person who was starved does not owe gratitude to the hunger for teaching them to appreciate food. Priya put it plainly once: she was a more compassionate, more discerning woman for what she'd survived — and she would trade every bit of that hard-won wisdom to have simply been treated well in the first place. Both halves of that sentence are true, and holding them together, refusing to collapse into either bitterness or false gratitude, is what honest meaning-making actually looks like.

In the end, this is the quiet triumph: a life built around your own values instead of their moods. For years, the organizing principle of your life was someone else's emotional weather — what would set them off, what would keep the peace, what they'd approve of. Freedom is when that organizing principle changes, when your days come to be shaped by what *you* value rather than by what someone else might feel. Imagine it: decisions made by your own compass, time spent on what matters to you, a life whose center of gravity has moved from managing them to expressing you. That's not selfishness; it's the ordinary birthright of a grown person, one that was taken from you and that you're now taking back. Renee described the strangeness, and then the deep rightness, of realizing she could make a major life decision without once asking how her mother would react — not out of defiance, just because her mother's reaction was genuinely no longer the axis her life turned on. That is what it means to become yourself. In the final chapter, we'll turn to the last frontier of that freedom — learning to let good people in, and to trust connection again without bracing for the old ache.

Chapter Twelve — Letting the Good Ones In

There's a cruel irony waiting at the end of this journey. You do the work, you get free, you rebuild yourself — and then the very safety you fought for asks something of you that feels impossible: to trust again. After everything, the idea of opening up to another person can feel less like hope and more like walking back toward the fire. *How do I ever let anyone in again without getting hurt?* Renee felt this acutely. She had learned to spot the danger, but she'd also grown so guarded that she was in danger of a different kind of loss — a safe, solitary life with the drawbridge permanently up. This final chapter of the twelve is about lowering it wisely: how to recognize the good ones, how to not recreate the old pattern, and what becomes possible on the other side. It's about the freedom this whole book is named for — the freedom that comes *after* them.

Recognizing Safe People

The first thing to learn is what healthy actually feels like — and the surprising news is that it often feels calm, even boring. If you were raised on chaos, calm can feel foreign, even suspect. The absence of drama can read as an absence of spark, because your nervous system was trained to equate intensity with love. So let me say this plainly, because it reorders everything: with a healthy person, you will not feel the dizzying highs and crushing lows you may have learned to call passion. You'll feel something steadier and, at first, almost disappointing — ease. Peace. The quiet of not having to brace. That flat, unremarkable steadiness is not the absence of love; it is what love feels like when it isn't laced with fear. Renee noticed she felt "nothing" with the calm, kind people, and slowly understood that the "nothing" was the absence of anxiety she'd always mistaken for the presence of feeling. Boring, it turns out, is the good news. Boring is safe. Boring is where a real life gets built.

Beyond the feeling, there are green flags you can learn to read as fluently as you once read red ones. Watch for consistency — the person who is the same on Tuesday as they were on Friday, whose warmth doesn't run hot and cold to keep you off balance. Watch for respect for your no, the small test of whether "no thank you" is honored or steamrolled. Watch, above all, for how they handle conflict, because this is the truest tell of all: a safe person can disagree with you, even be angry with you, and then *repair* — come back, own their part, restore the connection. This is the very thing you could never get from the toxic person, who only ever fought to win. With a healthy person, conflict is not a threat to the relationship; it's a normal event the relationship survives and even grows from. And watch for room — whether you can be fully yourself in their presence, opinions and quirks and needs intact, or whether you feel yourself shrinking to fit. Consistency, respect, repair, and room: learn those four, and you can read a person more reliably than any first-date chemistry ever told you.

And trust the good ones the way trust is actually meant to be built — in small increments, not handed over whole. Coming out of betrayal, people tend toward one of two extremes: they either bolt the doors entirely, or they fling them open and pour everything out at once, desperate for closeness, and get hurt again. Neither is real trust. Real trust is earned in stages, extended a little at a time and confirmed by how the person handles it. You share something small and see whether it's held with care. You watch whether their words and actions match over months, not moments. This is not paranoia; it's the ordinary, healthy pace of getting to know someone, the pace you were never taught because the toxic relationship demanded total loyalty up front. Letting trust be slow is not a wall. It's the difference between a drawbridge you can lower with discernment and a door that's either barricaded or flung wide. You get to be the one who decides, gradually, who has earned the next increment.

Not Repeating the Pattern

Beware that the familiar can masquerade as chemistry — and learn to tell the two apart. Here is the trap that catches even people who've done all this work: because your nervous system was shaped by a particular kind of person, that same kind can feel electric, magnetic, *right,* precisely because it's familiar. The charming intensity, the pursuit-and-withdrawal, the person who's a delightful project to win over — it can feel like destiny when it's actually just recognition. What you're feeling as "chemistry" may be your old wounds recognizing a familiar shape. This doesn't mean every strong attraction is a warning, but it does mean the *particular* pull toward someone who echoes the person who hurt you deserves suspicion rather than trust. Renee learned to notice when someone made her feel that old anxious spark — the butterflies that were really alarm bells — and to treat it not as a green light but as a reason to slow down and look harder. Sometimes the absence of that spark, with a steady and kind person, is the healthiest sign of all.

Renee met the test in the form of a man she was briefly, powerfully drawn to — charismatic, a little unpredictable, quick to adore her and quicker to go cool, so that she found herself, within weeks, working to win back his warmth. The pull was intoxicating, and that was exactly the problem. She recognized the choreography: the hot-and-cold rhythm that had trained her, as a girl, to chase a mother's approval. The intensity she felt was not the promise of love; it was the echo of an old wound being pressed. It took real discipline to walk away from something that felt so alive, because her whole system was screaming that alive was good. But she had learned, at last, to distrust that particular aliveness. What she chose instead — slower, steadier, less immediately thrilling — did not make her chest race. It made her chest *rest*. And she had lived long enough now to know which of those two feelings she could actually build a life on.

You also have to keep your boundaries with the healthy people too, not just the toxic ones. This surprises people. They assume boundaries are only for dangerous relationships and that with good people you can finally drop them entirely. But boundaries aren't weapons against bad people; they're the ordinary architecture of every healthy relationship. Good people *want* to know your limits, your needs, your no — it helps them love you well, and they don't punish you for having them. In fact, one quiet way to confirm someone is safe is to set a small boundary and watch: a healthy person receives it with respect, even gratitude, while a toxic one bristles or bulldozes. So keep practicing the skill you learned in Part Two, even now, even here. Boundaries don't disappear when the danger does. They simply become what they were always meant to be — not a shield, but a form of honesty between people who respect each other.

And now, for the first time, you get to have standards — to know when to give a chance and when to walk. Before, you had no floor; you accepted whatever you were given and called it love. Now you have a self to protect and a hard-won sense of what you will and won't live with, and that changes everything about how you choose. Not everyone deserves access to you, and that is not arrogance — it's the basic self-respect you were denied for so long. You can give people a fair chance and still keep your eyes open. You can walk away early, at the first stable sign of the old pattern, without needing to justify it to anyone or wait for proof that would cost you years. Renee found a strange new confidence in this: she no longer feared meeting another difficult person, because she finally trusted herself to recognize it fast and decline it early. The point of learning the pattern was never to live in fear of it. It was to be free of it — to move through the world of people with open eyes and a floor beneath your feet.

Freedom After Them

This is what it comes to: relationships as a place you can be at ease, not on guard. Remember where we began — the tightness in the chest, the bracing, the exhaustion of managing another person's moods. The opposite of that is the destination, and it's quieter than you might expect. It's being in a room with someone and feeling your shoulders drop. It's saying a hard thing and trusting it will be received. It's not rehearsing your words five times before you speak them. It's the profound, underrated luxury of not having to be careful. Renee marked her own arrival not by some grand event but by a small, almost unbearable sweetness: sitting at dinner with good friends, mid-laugh, and realizing that her chest was completely at ease, that she wasn't scanning anyone's face for a mood about to turn. She had forgotten a body could feel that way in company. That ease — ordinary, unremarkable, hard-won — is what safe love actually feels like.

It's worth pausing on how strange this ease can feel at first, because the strangeness trips people up. If you spent years on high alert, calm can register as emptiness, and safety as a kind of boredom you don't quite trust — you may even find yourself, out of old habit, creating small dramas just to feel the familiar charge. This is worth knowing in advance so you don't mistake it for a sign that something's missing. Nothing is missing. Your nervous system is simply learning a new baseline, and learning is slow. Give it time, and the calm stops feeling like a void and starts feeling like home. One day you'll notice you've stopped waiting for the other shoe to drop, not because you've grown careless, but because you've finally internalized that with this person, in this life, there is no other shoe. That is not naivety returning. It is safety, at long last, becoming believable.

Look, too, at what your life makes room for now that it isn't organized around them. All the energy you once poured into managing, appeasing, recovering — where does it go now? It goes to the people who actually love you back. It goes to the work you care about, the quiet mornings, the friendships that fill rather than drain, the version of you that had no room to exist before. This is the answer to the "no peace in solitude" worry that has run beneath this whole book: getting free of the toxic relationship was never about ending up alone. It was about clearing the space for everything and everyone good to finally come in. You removed the one drain so the whole garden could get water — and now, look, it's growing. The peace you found is not the peace of an empty room. It's the peace of a full one, finally full of the right people.

And here is the truth to carry out of these twelve chapters: you didn't just survive them. You're building something better than they ever let you have. Survival was the beginning, not the goal. What you're doing now is bigger — constructing a life richer, freer, and more genuinely yours than was ever possible in their shadow. The relationships you build now can have what the old one never could: honesty, safety, mutual respect, room to grow. That is not a consolation prize for what you lost. It is a better thing entirely, and you are its author. Renee, who once could not hear her mother's voice without her chest going tight, built a life full of people in whose company she could finally breathe — and kept, on her own careful terms, whatever limited contact with her mother she chose, no longer ruled by it either way. She had come full circle, and the circle closed somewhere new. That is freedom after them: not a life with no trace of what happened, but a life no longer governed by it — a life that is, at last, entirely your own. The twelve chapters end here. But there is one more thing, a thirteenth, and it belongs to you.

The Baker's Dozen — The Promise

A baker's dozen is thirteen — the extra one the baker adds, not because it's owed, but as a gift. Twelve chapters were mine to write. This thirteenth one is yours. It isn't another lesson; you've had enough lessons, and you've done the hard, brave work of living them. This is something different. It's a promise — a pledge you make to yourself, written out in full so you don't have to find the words on the days you'll need them most. Read it now, and then know where it lives, so you can come back to it whenever an old voice gets loud.

The Ground You've Covered

Look how far you've walked. In Part One, you learned to *see clearly* — that toxic is a pattern and a direction, not a single bad day; that their behavior was never your fault, even as you took honest ownership of your own; that the fog which hid it all was manufactured, and that staying as long as you did was survival, not weakness. In Part Two, you learned to *break free* — that a boundary is a line you keep for yourself, that distance is a dial and not only a switch, that guilt and grief are different and only one of them is trying to teach you something, that the pull to go back is withdrawal and it passes, and that the closure you waited for was always yours to give. And in Part Three, you began to *rebuild* — trusting your own mind again, meeting the self that went quiet to survive, and learning at last to let the good ones in.

That's not a small thing you did. That's a whole life, reclaimed. Hold onto the through-line of all of it: you are not to blame for how you were treated, and you are responsible for what you do now — and that responsibility was never a burden. It was your power, handed back to you.

Where They Are Now

You walked this road with some company, so let's see them off. Renee kept her mother in her life on her own careful terms — lunches in public, on good days, with the door to her heart guarded but not bolted — and built around that a life so full of steady, loving people that her mother became, at last, a minor character in it. Priya, long free of Dev, rediscovered a woman she'd forgotten she was, and learned to trust the calm. Theo left the boss whose praise he'd been starving for and found work that didn't require him to bleed for scraps. Marcus discovered that when he stopped rescuing, some friendships thinned to nothing and the real ones grew — and made his peace with both. And Daniel, who chose the hardest road of all, lived quietly and well beyond his father's reach, wishing the man peace from a safe distance and refusing, gently, to hand his own children a danger he'd barely survived. Different rooms, different roads. The same freedom, at the end of each.

The Pledge

Here is the promise. Read it slowly, and out loud if you can — there's something about hearing your own voice say these words that makes them take. It's written as *I*, because it's yours now.

I am leaving behind the belief that I must earn love by shrinking, and the habit of apologizing for someone else's behavior. I am leaving behind the exhausting hope that if I could only be good enough, they would finally be who I needed. That hope kept me waiting for years. I set it down.

I will no longer accept contempt dressed as honesty, control dressed as love, or cruelty dressed as "just how they are." I will no longer trade my peace for a quiet that only I am asked to keep. I know now that a relationship should cost roughly what it gives, and I will pay attention to the ledger.

I will speak to myself the way I would speak to someone I love — honestly, and without contempt. I will let myself be corrected, because I am not too proud to grow: if I cannot be corrected without being offended, then I will never grow, and I intend to keep growing until the day I die. But I will know the difference between correction, which is aimed at what I did and leaves me steadier, and contempt, which is aimed at who I am and leaves me smaller. I will accept the first and refuse the second, from others and from myself.

I will remember that I am not to blame for how I was treated, and that I am responsible for what I do next. I will hold both. I will not become the villain of my own story by pretending I was a flawless victim, and I will not carry blame that was never mine to carry. I will keep the honest middle — the only ground worth standing on.

I will protect my peace, even from people I love. I will keep my boundaries with the good people too, because that is what honesty between equals looks like. And I will let the good ones in, slowly, an increment at a time, trusting calm over chaos and choosing the person who lets my chest rest over the one who makes it race.

When the Old Voice Gets Loud

You will have hard days. This is not a door you walk through once; it's a road you walk many times, and some days you'll find yourself back at the start of it. That is not failure. Going back in your mind for a moment isn't losing your progress — it's part of healing, and you simply come back here. This page is the place you come back to.

When the pull comes — when you miss them so much it aches, when a warm message arrives right as you were finally steady — remember that this is withdrawal, not truth, and that it always crests and passes. You don't have to decide anything tonight. Open your honesty list. Call a good person. Wait for morning before you trust anything the longing says.

When the guilt comes — when the chorus of "but they're family, how could you, you're selfish" starts up inside you — stop and ask whose voice that actually is. Ask whether this is guilt, which means you did something wrong, or grief, which just means it hurts. Grief is not corrected by going back. And you never needed anyone's permission to protect yourself.

When the self-doubt comes — when you second-guess your own memory, your own read, your own right to have left — remember that your compass was never broken, only distrusted. You saw what you saw. You felt what you felt. You are allowed to be the authority on your own life.

Permission to Wobble

Grant yourself this, in advance, for the days you'll need it: you are allowed to have hard days. You are allowed to miss them, to doubt yourself, to wobble, to cry in the car and not know if it's grief or relief. None of that undoes what you've built. Healing is not a straight line and it was never going to be. The measure of your progress is not that the old voice went silent — it's that you learned to recognize it, and to come back to yourself a little faster each time. Wobbling is not falling. It's what walking looks like, up close.

Freedom After Them

So here, at the end, is the extra one — the thirteenth, the gift. You didn't just survive them. You saw clearly, you broke free, you rebuilt, and you are building something better than they ever let you have: a life that is at ease instead of on guard, full of the right people, organized around what you value instead of what someone else might feel. That life is yours now, and no one can cast you back into a role you've refused to play.

Come back to this page whenever you need it. Read the pledge again on the hard days. And on the good ones — the ordinary, unremarkable, hard-won good ones, when your shoulders drop in someone's company and you realize you've stopped waiting for the other shoe to fall — let yourself notice that this, finally, is what you fought for. This is freedom after them. It was always going to be yours. Welcome home.

About the Author

Cain Baker writes gentle, honest books for people doing hard inner work. His writing began with *The Weightless Home*, a guide to releasing the physical and emotional clutter we carry, and the same spirit runs through everything since: warm, plain-spoken, and free of jargon, but never soft on the truth. He believes that real healing respects the reader — that people are capable of accountability as well as compassion, and that the kindest thing an author can do is tell you the truth in a voice you can actually bear to hear.

Freedom After Them grew out of a conviction that the conversation around toxic relationships had drifted to two unhelpful extremes: one that excuses every hurt as unforgivable abuse, and another that shames anyone who dares to step back from family. He wanted to write the book that lives in the honest middle — that takes your pain seriously, hands you your own agency, and refuses to pretend that either staying or leaving is always the answer.

He writes under a pen name because he cares more about the words being useful than about being known. If this book helped you, that is the only signature he was ever after.

A Small Ask

If *Freedom After Them* met you where you were, would you consider leaving an honest review wherever you bought it? Reviews are how quiet books find the next person who needs them — someone, right now, keeping a list in their head and wondering if they're crazy. A few words from you might be the thing that reaches them. Thank you for reading, and for the courage it took to do the work these pages describe.

Also by Cain Baker

The Weightless Home — a gentle guide to releasing the clutter we carry, in our spaces and in ourselves, and making room for a lighter way of living.

A Word on Getting Help

This book is a companion, not a substitute for professional care. Healing from a toxic relationship can stir up grief, anxiety, and depression, and there is no weakness in seeking a good therapist or counselor to walk alongside you.

And if your situation is not only toxic but unsafe — if you are being threatened, controlled, or physically hurt — please reach for help built for exactly that. In the United States, the National Domestic Violence Hotline is free, confidential, and available around the clock: call 1-800-799-SAFE (7233), text START to 88788, or chat at thehotline.org. If you are outside the United States, an internet search for "domestic violence hotline" plus your country will find the equivalent. And if you are ever in immediate danger, contact your local emergency number. Reaching out is not an overreaction. It is the same clear-eyed courage this whole book is about.

www.ingramcontent.com/pod-product-compliance
Lightning Source LLC
LaVergne TN
LVHW030727061126
851857LV00019B/2026
9798997030568

instant, the function always vanishes. Stokes[1]) objects to this method of proof as not rigorous inasmuch as it is not evident that the functions ξ, η, ζ can be developed by Taylor's theorem, and replaces it by the following demonstration.

Let L be a superior limit to the numerical values of the coefficients of $\frac{\xi}{\varrho}, \frac{\eta}{\varrho}, \frac{\zeta}{\varrho}$ in the second member of equations 57). Then evidently ξ, η, ζ cannot increase faster than if their numerical or absolute values satisfied the equations

58) $$\begin{aligned} \frac{d}{dt}\left|\frac{\xi}{\varrho}\right| &= L\left(\left|\frac{\xi}{\varrho}\right| + \left|\frac{\eta}{\varrho}\right| + \left|\frac{\zeta}{\varrho}\right|\right), \\ \frac{d}{dt}\left|\frac{\eta}{\varrho}\right| &= L\left(\left|\frac{\xi}{\varrho}\right| + \left|\frac{\eta}{\varrho}\right| + \left|\frac{\zeta}{\varrho}\right|\right), \\ \frac{d}{dt}\left|\frac{\zeta}{\varrho}\right| &= L\left(\left|\frac{\xi}{\varrho}\right| + \left|\frac{\eta}{\varrho}\right| + \left|\frac{\zeta}{\varrho}\right|\right), \end{aligned}$$

instead of 57), ξ, η, ζ vanishing in this case also when $t=0$. Adding these three equations and writing

$$\left|\frac{\xi}{\varrho}\right| + \left|\frac{\eta}{\varrho}\right| + \left|\frac{\zeta}{\varrho}\right| = \Omega,$$

we obtain

59) $$\frac{d\Omega}{dt} = L\Omega.$$

The integral of this equation is

$$\Omega = ce^{Lt},$$

and since $\Omega = 0$ when $t = 0$, c must be zero, and Ω is always zero. Since the sum of the absolute values cannot vanish unless the separate values vanish, the theorem is proved.

Let us now consider two points A and B lying on the same vortex line at a distance apart $ds = \varepsilon \frac{\omega}{\varrho}$, where ε is a small constant. Since the particles lie on a vortex-line we have

60) $$\frac{dx}{\xi} = \frac{dy}{\eta} = \frac{dz}{\zeta} = \frac{ds}{\omega} = \frac{\varepsilon}{\varrho}.$$

We have for the difference of velocity at A and B

61) $$\begin{aligned} u_B - u_A &= \frac{\partial u}{\partial x}dx + \frac{\partial u}{\partial y}dy + \frac{\partial u}{\partial z}dz \\ &= \varepsilon\left\{\frac{\xi}{\varrho}\frac{\partial u}{\partial x} + \frac{\eta}{\varrho}\frac{\partial u}{\partial y} + \frac{\zeta}{\varrho}\frac{\partial u}{\partial z}\right\}, \end{aligned}$$

or by equations 57),

62) $$u_B - u_A = \varepsilon\frac{d}{dt}\left(\frac{\xi}{\varrho}\right).$$

---

1) Stokes, *Math. and Phys. Papers*, Vol. II, p. 36.

Now at an instant later by dt, when the particles are at A' and B', we have

$$\begin{aligned} &dx' = dx + (u_B - u_A)\, dt = \varepsilon\left[\frac{\xi}{\varrho} + \frac{d}{dt}\left(\frac{\xi}{\varrho}\right) dt\right], \\ 63)\qquad &dy' = dy + (u_B - u_A)\, dt = \varepsilon\left[\frac{\eta}{\varrho} + \frac{d}{dt}\left(\frac{\eta}{\varrho}\right) dt\right], \\ &dz' = dz + (u_B - u_A)\, dt = \varepsilon\left[\frac{\zeta}{\varrho} + \frac{d}{dt}\left(\frac{\zeta}{\varrho}\right) dt\right]. \end{aligned}$$

Therefore the projections of the arc ds' in the new position are proportional to the new values of $\frac{\xi}{\varrho}, \frac{\eta}{\varrho}, \frac{\zeta}{\varrho}$, as they originally were, so that the particles still lie on a vortex-line. Accordingly a vortex-line is always composed of the same particles of fluid. Also since the components of ds have increased or have changed so as to be always proportional to the components of $\frac{\omega}{\varrho}$, if the liquid is incompressible the rotation is proportional to the distance between the particles. And whether ϱ vary or not, if S be the area of the cross-section of a vortex-filament, $\varrho S ds$, the mass of a length ds remaining constant, so does $S\omega$, the strength of the filament.

It is easy to see that this is equivalent to a statement of the conservation of angular momentum for each portion of the fluid. Evidently in a perfect fluid no moment can be exerted on any portion, since the tangential forces vanish.

Accordingly the strength of a vortex-filament is constant, not only at all points in the filament but at all times, consequently a vortex existing in a perfect fluid is indestructible, however it may move. It is from this remarkable property of vortices discovered by Helmholtz that Lord Kelvin was lead to imagine atoms as consisting of vortices in a perfect fluid.

192. Vector Potential. Helmholtz's Theorem. We have seen that any curl is a solenoidal vector. We may naturally ask whether conversely any solenoidal vector can be replaced by the curl of another vector. It was shown by Helmholtz that any uniform continuous vector point-function vanishing at infinity can be expressed as the sum of a lamellar and a solenoidal part, and the solenoidal part may be expressed as the curl of a vector point-function. A vector point-function is completely determined if its divergence and curl are everywhere given. Let q be the given vector, which in our case is the velocity of the fluid. Let us suppose that it is possible to express it as the sum of the vector-parameter of a scalar func-

tion φ and the curl of a vector function Q, whose components are U, V, W. Accordingly let us put

64)
$$u = \frac{\partial \varphi}{\partial x} + \frac{\partial W}{\partial y} - \frac{\partial V}{\partial z},$$
$$v = \frac{\partial \varphi}{\partial y} + \frac{\partial U}{\partial z} - \frac{\partial W}{\partial x},$$
$$w = \frac{\partial \varphi}{\partial z} + \frac{\partial V}{\partial x} - \frac{\partial U}{\partial y}.$$

Finding first the divergence of q we have

65)
$$\text{div.}\, q = \frac{\partial u}{\partial x} + \frac{\partial v}{\partial y} + \frac{\partial w}{\partial z} = \varDelta\varphi,$$

the divergence of the curl part vanishing. But by § 128, 5) we know that if φ and its first derivatives are everywhere finite and continuous, we have

66)
$$\varphi = -\frac{1}{4\pi}\iiint_{\infty} \frac{\varDelta\varphi}{r}\, d\tau = -\frac{1}{4\pi}\iiint_{\infty} \frac{\text{div.}\, q}{r}\, d\tau.$$

Since q is continuous by hypothesis, div. q is finite. Consequently the lamellar part of q is determined by its divergence.

Secondly finding the curl of q,

67)
$$2\xi = \frac{\partial w}{\partial y} - \frac{\partial v}{\partial z} = \frac{\partial}{\partial y}\left(\frac{\partial \varphi}{\partial z} + \frac{\partial V}{\partial x} - \frac{\partial U}{\partial y}\right) - \frac{\partial}{\partial z}\left(\frac{\partial \varphi}{\partial y} + \frac{\partial U}{\partial z} - \frac{\partial W}{\partial x}\right)$$
$$= -\varDelta U + \frac{\partial}{\partial x}\left(\frac{\partial U}{\partial x} + \frac{\partial V}{\partial y} + \frac{\partial W}{\partial z}\right).$$

Since the vector Q is as yet undetermined except as to its partial derivatives by equations 64), let us assume that it is solenoidal, or

68)
$$\frac{\partial U}{\partial x} + \frac{\partial V}{\partial y} + \frac{\partial W}{\partial z} = 0,$$

then we have

69)
$$2\xi = -\varDelta U,$$
$$2\eta = -\varDelta V,$$
$$2\zeta = -\varDelta W,$$

the integrals of which are as above,

70)
$$U = \frac{1}{2\pi}\iiint \frac{\xi}{r}\, d\tau,$$
$$V = \frac{1}{2\pi}\iiint \frac{\eta}{r}\, d\tau,$$
$$W = \frac{1}{2\pi}\iiint \frac{\zeta}{r}\, d\tau.$$

Where the vorticity vanishes the space contributes nothing to the integrals, so that the latter may be taken over all the vortices. Thus we see that Q, which determines the solenoidal part of q, is determined by curl q. Consequently both parts of q are completely determined and the theorem is proved. If q is solenoidal div. q vanishes, $\varphi = 0$, and $q = \text{curl}\, Q$. Accordingly every solenoidal vector may be represented as a curl. If q is irrotational curl $q = 0$ and $Q = 0$, so that every irrotational vector is lamellar, as we saw in § 31.

The vector Q, whose *components* are formed as potential functions for densities $\frac{\xi}{2\pi}, \frac{\eta}{2\pi}, \frac{\zeta}{2\pi}$ respectively, is called the *vector potential* of the vector $\frac{\omega}{2\pi}$. We may thus abbreviate our results in the vector equations,

71) $$\bar{q} = \text{vector parameter } \varphi + \text{curl } \bar{Q},$$

72) $$\varphi = -\frac{1}{4\pi}\iiint\limits_{\infty} \frac{\text{div. } q}{r}\, d\tau,$$

73) $$\bar{Q} = \frac{1}{4\pi}\iiint\limits_{\infty} \frac{\text{curl } q}{r}\, d\tau.$$

Let us verify that $\bar{Q}$ as determined is solenoidal. We shall distinguish the point of integration by accents, so that

70) $$U = \frac{1}{2\pi}\iiint \frac{\xi'}{r}\, d\tau', \quad V = \frac{1}{2\pi}\iiint \frac{\eta'}{r}\, d\tau', \quad W = \frac{1}{2\pi}\iiint \frac{\zeta'}{r}\, d\tau',$$

$$r^2 = (x - x')^2 + (y - y')^2 + (z - z')^2.$$

Differentiating we have

74) $$\frac{\partial U}{\partial x} = \frac{1}{2\pi}\iiint \xi' \frac{\partial}{\partial x}\left(\frac{1}{r}\right) d\tau' = -\frac{1}{2\pi}\iiint \xi' \frac{\partial}{\partial x'}\left(\frac{1}{r}\right) d\tau'$$
$$= \frac{1}{2\pi}\left[\iint \frac{\xi'}{r} \cos(nx)\, dS + \iiint \frac{1}{r}\frac{\partial \xi'}{\partial x'}\, d\tau'\right].$$

In like manner

75) $$\frac{\partial U}{\partial x} + \frac{\partial V}{\partial y} + \frac{\partial W}{\partial z}$$
$$= \frac{1}{2\pi}\left[\iint \left(\xi' \cos(nx) + \eta' \cos(ny) + \zeta' \cos(nz)\right)\frac{dS}{r} + \iiint \frac{1}{r}\left(\frac{\partial \xi'}{\partial x'} + \frac{\partial \eta'}{\partial y'} + \frac{\partial \zeta'}{\partial z'}\right) d\tau'\right].$$

But since ω is solenoidal the volume integral vanishes, and, since at the surface of the vortices, which are composed of vortex-lines, ω is tangential, the surface integral vanishes and div. $Q = 0$.

193. Velocity due to Vortex. Let us now consider in an incompressible fluid the velocity at any point due to vortical motion. We have

$$76)\quad u = \frac{\partial W}{\partial y} - \frac{\partial V}{\partial z} = \frac{1}{2\pi}\left[\frac{\partial}{\partial y}\left(\iiint \frac{\zeta'}{r}\, d\tau'\right) - \frac{\partial}{\partial z}\left(\iiint \frac{\eta'}{r}\, d\tau'\right)\right]$$
$$= \frac{1}{2\pi}\iiint\left\{\zeta' \frac{\partial}{\partial y}\left(\frac{1}{r}\right) - \eta' \frac{\partial}{\partial z}\left(\frac{1}{r}\right)\right\} d\tau'.$$

Thus the portions of the velocity contributed by an element $d\tau'$ of the vortex are:

$$du = \frac{1}{2\pi r^2}\left\{\zeta'\left(\frac{y'-y}{r}\right) - \eta'\left(\frac{z'-z}{r}\right)\right\} d\tau',$$

$$77)\quad dv = \frac{1}{2\pi r^2}\left\{\xi'\left(\frac{z'-z}{r}\right) - \zeta'\left(\frac{x'-x}{r}\right)\right\} d\tau',$$

$$dw = \frac{1}{2\pi r^2}\left\{\eta'\left(\frac{x'-x}{r}\right) - \xi'\left(\frac{y'-y}{r}\right)\right\} d\tau',$$

or the velocity at the point x, y, z due to the element $d\tau'$ is $\frac{1}{2\pi r^3}$ multiplied by the vector-product of the vorticity and the vector r drawn from the element $d\tau'$ of the vortex to the point x, y, z. If dq be the magnitude of the resultant of du, dv, dw we thus have

$$78)\qquad dq = \frac{\omega \sin(\omega, r)}{2\pi r^2}\, d\tau'.$$

Let us take for the element $d\tau'$ a length ds of a vortex filament of cross-section S. Then $d\tau' = S ds$ and since $S\omega = \varkappa$, the strength of the filament,

$$79)\qquad dq = \frac{\varkappa\, ds \sin(\omega, r)}{2\pi r^2}.$$

The velocity is connected with the vorticity in the same may that the magnetic field is connected with the electric current density producing it, and equation 79) gives us the magnetic field produced by a linear current element of length ds and strength $\frac{\varkappa}{2\pi}$.[1])

1) See the author's treatise on *The Theory of Electricity and Magnetism*, §§ 222—226.

194. Kinetic Energy of Vortex. The kinetic energy of the incompressible liquid moving vortically is

$$80)\quad T = \frac{1}{2}\varrho\iiint(u^2+v^2+w^2)\,d\tau$$
$$= \frac{\varrho}{2}\iiint\left[u\left(\frac{\partial W}{\partial y}-\frac{\partial V}{\partial z}\right)+v\left(\frac{\partial U}{\partial z}-\frac{\partial W}{\partial x}\right)+w\left(\frac{\partial V}{\partial x}-\frac{\partial U}{\partial y}\right)\right]d\tau$$
$$= \frac{\varrho}{2}\iint[(vW-wV)\cos(nx)+(wU-uW)\cos(ny)$$
$$+(uV-vU)\cos(nz)]\,dS$$
$$+\frac{\varrho}{2}\iiint\left[U\left(\frac{\partial w}{\partial y}-\frac{\partial v}{\partial z}\right)+V\left(\frac{\partial u}{\partial z}-\frac{\partial w}{\partial x}\right)+W\left(\frac{\partial v}{\partial x}-\frac{\partial u}{\partial y}\right)\right]d\tau.$$

If the integral be taken over all space, since the motion is supposed to vanish at infinity the surface integrals vanish, and

$$81)\qquad T = \varrho\iiint[U\xi+V\eta+W\zeta]\,d\tau,$$

or inserting the values of U, V, W from 70)

$$82)\qquad T = \frac{\varrho}{2\pi}\iiiint\!\!\iint\frac{\xi\xi'+\eta\eta'+\zeta\zeta'}{r}\,d\tau\,d\tau',$$

and the integration may now be restricted to the vortices.

If again we integrate by filaments, we find

$$83)\qquad T = \frac{\varrho}{2\pi}\iiiint\!\!\iint\frac{\varkappa\varkappa'\cos(ds,ds')}{r}\,ds\,ds',$$

where the integration is expressed as over the length of each of the double infinity of vortex-filaments constituting the vortices. This is the form obtained for the energy of two electric currents by Franz Neumann.

195. Straight parallel Vortices. Let us now consider the case in which the vorticity is everywhere parallel to a single direction, that of the axis of z. Let the motion be uniplanar, that is parallel to a single plane, the XY-plane, and the same in all planes parallel to it. All quantities are therefore independent of z. The vortices are columnar and either of infinite length or end at the free surface of the liquid. Such vortices may be produced standing vertically in a tank with a horizontal bottom. Under the conditions imposed we have

$$84)\qquad 0 = w = \frac{\partial u}{\partial z} = \frac{\partial v}{\partial z} = \frac{\partial w}{\partial z} = \xi = \eta = U = V,$$

and

$$85)\qquad u = \frac{\partial W}{\partial y},\quad v = -\frac{\partial W}{\partial x},$$

$$86)\qquad 2\zeta = \frac{\partial v}{\partial x} - \frac{\partial u}{\partial y},$$

and by equations 57)

$$\frac{d\zeta}{dt} = 0,$$

so that ζ is independent of the time for any given vortex-filament.

The function W is not a velocity potential, but is said to be *conjugate* to a velocity potential φ for which

$$87)\qquad u = \frac{\partial \varphi}{\partial x}, \quad v = \frac{\partial \varphi}{\partial y}.$$

The function W has a simple physical meaning. If we find the amount of liquid which flows across a cylindrical surface with generators parallel to the z-axis of height unity in unit of time, we have

$$88)\qquad \psi = \int_A^B q \cos(qn)\, ds = \int_A^B [u \cos(nx) + v \cos(ny)]\, ds,$$

the line integral being taken around any orthogonal section of the cylinder. Now we have

$$ds \cos(nx) = \quad dy,$$
$$ds \cos(ny) = -\, dx,$$

so that

$$89)\qquad \psi = \int (u\,dy - v\,dx) = \int_A^B \left(\frac{\partial W}{\partial x} dx + \frac{\partial W}{\partial y} dy\right) = W_B - W_A.$$

A function, the difference of whose values at two points A and B gives the quantity flowing in unit time across a cylinder of unit height drawn on any curve with ends at A and B, is called a flux or current function. The quantity crossing is independent of the curve because the fluid is incompressible. In the present case the vector potential W is a current function. The stream lines being lines across which no current flows are given by the equation $\psi = const.$ Substituting the values of u and v from 85) in 86), we have

$$90)\qquad -2\zeta = \frac{\partial^2 W}{\partial x^2} + \frac{\partial^2 W}{\partial y^2}.$$

But this is the equation for a logarithmic potential with density $\frac{\zeta}{\pi}$, § 138, 61), so that we have as the integral

$$91)\qquad W = -\frac{1}{\pi}\iint \zeta' \log r\, dS',$$

as may also be found from equation 70) by integrating over the infinite cylinder as in § 135, subject to the difficulty mentioned on p. 385. The value of W given in equation 91) satisfies the equation

92) $$\frac{\partial^2 W}{\partial x^2} + \frac{\partial^2 W}{\partial y^2} = 0$$

outside of the vortices and equation 90) at points within them, as shown in § 138. If we have a single vortex filament of cross-section dS and strength $\varkappa = \zeta' dS$,

93) $$W = -\frac{\zeta'}{\pi} \log r\, dS = -\frac{\varkappa}{\pi} \log r,$$

and the lines of flow are circles, $r = const.$ Then

94) $$u = \frac{\partial W}{\partial y} = \frac{\varkappa}{\pi r} \cdot \frac{y' - y}{r}, \qquad v = -\frac{\partial W}{\partial x} = \frac{\varkappa}{\pi r} \cdot \frac{x - x'}{r},$$

95) $$q^2 = u^2 + v^2 = \frac{\varkappa^2}{\pi^2 r^2},$$

the velocity is perpendicular to the radius joining the point x, y with the vortex and inversely proportional to its length. It is to be observed that although the motion is whirling, every point describing a circle about the center, the motion is irrotational except at the center, where the vortex-filament is situated, each particle describing its path without turning about itself, like a body of soldiers obliquing or changing direction while each man faces in the same unchanging direction. The motion in the vortex on the contrary is similar to that of a body of soldiers *wheeling* or changing direction like a rigid body rotating.

If we have a number of vortices of strengths $\varkappa_1, \varkappa_2, \ldots \varkappa_n$, and form the linear functions of the velocities of each,

96) $$U = \Sigma \varkappa_s u_s,\text{[1]} \qquad V = \Sigma \varkappa_s v_s,$$

where u_s, v_s, is the velocity at the vortex s both vanish. For any pair of vortices r and s we have

$$u_r = \varkappa_s \cdot \frac{x_s - x_r}{\pi r^2},$$

where u_r is the part of the velocity at x_r, y_r due to the vortex of strength $\varkappa_s$ situated at $x_s y_s$. Thus

$$\varkappa_r u_r = \varkappa_s \varkappa_r \cdot \frac{x_s - x_r}{\pi r^2},$$

while similarly

$$\varkappa_s u_s = \varkappa_s \varkappa_r \frac{x_r - x_s}{\pi r^2},$$

so that the terms of the sum destroy each other in pairs.

1) U and V have nothing here to do with the components of the vector-potential.

Similarly for vortices continuously distributed, the strength of any elementary filament being ζdS,

$$97)\qquad U = \iint u\zeta dS = \iiiint \zeta\zeta' \cdot \frac{x'-x}{r} \cdot dS\,dS',$$

which again vanishes, since every point is covered by both dS and dS'.

If we define the center of the vortex as $x_0 y_0$ where

$$98)\qquad \begin{aligned} x_0 \iint \zeta dS &= \iint x\zeta dS, \\ y_0 \iint \zeta dS &= \iint y\zeta dS, \end{aligned}$$

then since ζ does not depend upon t, if we follow the particle differentiating,

$$99)\qquad \frac{dx_0}{dt} \iint \zeta dS = \iint u\zeta dS = 0,$$

the integrals being taken over areas moving with the liquid. Therefore

$$100)\qquad \frac{dx_0}{dt} = \frac{dy_0}{dt} = 0,$$

or the center of all columnar vortices present remains at rest.

If we have a single vortex filament of infinitesimal cross-section S, for which

$$101)\qquad \iint \zeta dS = \varkappa,$$

the velocity depends on the current function $W = -\frac{\varkappa}{\pi}\log r$. In the vortex and close to it, if $\varkappa$ is finite, ζ, W, u, v are infinite. But at the center $u = v = 0$, the vortex stands still and the fluid moves about it in circles with velocity $\frac{\varkappa}{\pi r}$. The angular velocity and the area of the cross-section remain constant, although the shape of the latter may vary. If we have two such vortex-filaments each urges the other in a direction perpendicular to the line joining them, they accordingly revolve about their center, maintaining a constant distance from each other. If they are whirling in the same direction the center is between them (Fig. 162), but if in opposite directions, it is outside, and if they are equal it lies at infinity. Such a pair of vortices may be called a vortex-couple or doublet, and they advance at a constant velocity, keeping symmetrical with respect to the plane bisecting perpendicularly the line joining them. This plane is a stream-plane and may accordingly be taken as a boundary of the

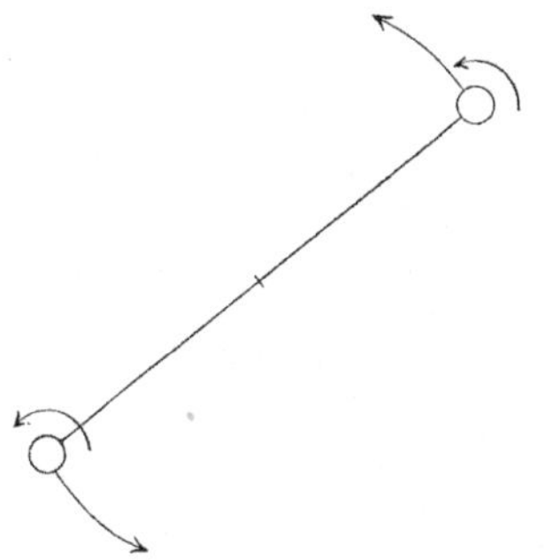

Fig. 162.

fluid. Since either vortex moves with a velocity $\frac{\varkappa}{\pi r}$ and half way between them the velocity being due to both is $\frac{2\varkappa}{\frac{\pi r}{2}} = \frac{4\varkappa}{\pi r}$, we find that a single vortex near a plane wall moves parallel to it with a velocity one fourth that of the water at the wall. This is an illustration of the method of images, of frequent application in hydrodynamics.

As another illustration consider the motion of a single vortex-filament in a square corner inclosed by two infinite walls. The motion is evidently the same as if we had a pair of vortex-couples formed by the given vortex and its images in the two walls, turning as shown in Fig. 163 and forming what may be called a vortex kaleidoscope.

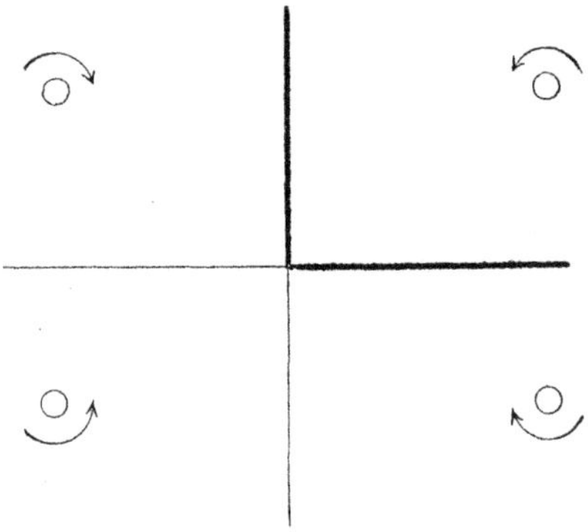

Fig. 163.

From the symmetry it is evident that the planes of the walls are stream-planes, so that we may consider the motion in one corner alone. If x and y be the coordinates of the vortex considered, we have as due to the others,

102) $$u = \frac{\varkappa}{2\pi y} - \frac{\varkappa}{2\pi} \cdot \frac{y}{x^2+y^2} = \frac{\varkappa}{2\pi} \frac{x^2}{y(x^2+y^2)},$$
$$v = -\frac{\varkappa}{2\pi x} + \frac{\varkappa}{2\pi} \frac{x}{x^2+y^2} = -\frac{\varkappa}{2\pi} \frac{y^2}{x(x^2+y^2)}.$$

Since u and v are the velocities $\frac{dx}{dt}, \frac{dy}{dt}$ of the vortex, we have for the equation of its path

103) $$\frac{\frac{dx}{dt}}{\frac{dy}{dt}} = \frac{u}{v} = -\frac{x^3}{y^3} = \frac{dx}{dy}, \text{ or}$$
$$\frac{dx}{x^3} = -\frac{dy}{y^3},$$

whose integral is

104) $$\frac{1}{x^2} + \frac{1}{y^2} = \frac{1}{a^2}, \quad x^2 + y^2 = \frac{x^2 y^2}{a^2},$$

and in polar coordinates,

$$r^2 = \frac{r^4}{a^2} \sin^2 \vartheta \cos^2 \vartheta,$$

105) $$r \sin 2\vartheta = \pm 2a,$$

the equation of a Cotes's spiral, having one of the axes as an asymptote.

The same problem gives us the motion of two equal vortex-couples approaching each other head on, or a single vortex-couple approaching a plane boundary, showing how as they are stopped they spread out. The beharior of vortex-couples will serve to illustrate that of circular vortex rings, for the theory of which the reader is referred to Helmholtz's original paper. The two opposite parts of a circular vortex appear to be rotating in opposite directions if viewed on their intersection by a diametral plane normal to the circle, thus resembling a vortex-couple. It is found that the circular vortex advances with a constant velocity in the direction of the fluid in the center, maintaining its diameter, but that when approaching a wall head on it spreads out like the vortex-couple. Two circular vortices approaching each other do the same thing, but if moving in the same direction the forward one spreads out, the following one contracts and is sucked through the foremost vortex, when it in turn spreads out and the one which is now behind passes through it, and so on in turn, as may also be shown for two columnar vortex-couples traveling in the same direction.

Most of these properties of circular vortices may be realized with smoke rings made by causing smoke to puff out through a circular hole in a box, or mouth of a smoker, or smoke-stack of a locomotive. The friction at the edge of the hole holds the outside of the smoke back, while the inside goes forward, establishing thereby the vortical rotation. As previously stated no vortex could be formed if there were no friction. It is to be noticed that the direction of the fluid on the *inside* of the vortex gives the direction of advance.

196. Irrotational Motion. We shall now consider the non-vortical motion of an incompressible fluid. We then have a velocity potential φ and

106) $$u = \frac{\partial \varphi}{\partial x}, \quad v = \frac{\partial \varphi}{\partial y}, \quad w = \frac{\partial \varphi}{\partial z}.$$

The equation of continuity becomes

107) $$\Delta \varphi = 0,$$

and the potential is harmonic at all points except where liquid is being created (*sources*) or withdrawn (*sinks*). The volume of flow per unit time outward from any closed surface S is

108) $$-\iint [u \cos(nx) + v \cos(ny) + w \cos(nz)]\, dS$$
$$= -\iint \frac{\partial \varphi}{\partial n}\, dS = \iiint \Delta \varphi\, d\tau,$$

so that if this is not equal to zero, it is equal to the quantity created in the space considered in unit time,

$$109)\qquad \frac{dQ}{dt} = \iiint \Delta\varphi\, d\tau,$$

so that if we put $\Delta\varphi = \sigma$, σ is the amount of liquid produced per unit volume per unit of time. The total amount

$$\frac{dQ}{dt} = \iiint \sigma\, d\tau$$

is called the *strength of the source.* If σ is given as a function of the point we have

$$110)\qquad \varphi = -\frac{1}{4\pi}\iiint \frac{\Delta\varphi}{r}\, d\tau = -\frac{1}{4\pi}\iiint \frac{\sigma}{r}\, d\tau.$$

Accordingly the velocity potential has the properties of a force potential, the density of attracting matter being represented by $\frac{1}{4\pi}$ times the strength of source per unit volume. The negative sign occurs here from the different convention employed, it being customary to define the force as the negative parameter, the velocity as the positive parameter of its potential. In particular a point source of strength m produces a radial velocity of magnitude $\frac{1}{4\pi}\frac{m}{r^2}$. This system is called by Clifford a *squirt.*

197. Uniplanar Motion. A simple and interesting case is that of uniplanar flow as defined above. We then have all quantities independent of z, so that Laplace's equation reduces to

$$111)\qquad \frac{\partial^2\varphi}{\partial x^2} + \frac{\partial^2\varphi}{\partial y^2} = 0.$$

A powerful method of treatment of such problems is furnished by the method of functions of a complex variable. The complex number $a + ib$, where a and b are real numbers and i is a unit defined by the equation

$$i^2 = -1,$$

(the same root being always taken) is subject to all the laws of algebra, and vanishes only when a and b both vanish separately. Any function of the complex number obtained by algebraic operations, after substituting for every factor i^2 its value -1, becomes the sum of a real number plus a pure imaginary, that is a real number multiplied by i. Any equation between complex numbers is equivalent to two equations between real numbers, being satisfied only when the real parts in both numbers are equal as well as the real coefficients of i in both members. If z denote the complex variable $x + iy$, any function of z may be written

$$w = f(z) = u + iv,$$

where u and v are real functions of the two real variables x and y. For instance

112) $$z^2 = (x + iy)^2 = x^2 - y^2 + 2ixy, \quad u = x^2 - y^2, \quad v = 2xy,$$

113) $$\frac{1}{z} = \frac{1}{x + iy} = \frac{x - iy}{x^2 + y^2} = \frac{x}{x^2 + y^2} - \frac{iy}{x^2 + y^2}, \quad u = \frac{x}{x^2 + y^2}, \quad v = -\frac{y}{x^2 + y^2}.$$

Let us examine the relation between an infinitesimal change in z and the corresponding change in $f(z)$. We have, x and y being real variables capable of independent variation,

114) $$dz = dx + i\,dy,$$

115) $$df(z) = dw = du + i\,dv = \frac{\partial u}{\partial x}dx + \frac{\partial u}{\partial y}dy + i\left(\frac{\partial v}{\partial x}dx + \frac{\partial v}{\partial y}dy\right).$$

Consequently by division,

116) $$\frac{dw}{dz} = \frac{du + i\,dv}{dx + i\,dy} = \frac{\frac{\partial u}{\partial x}dx + \frac{\partial u}{\partial y}dy + i\left(\frac{\partial v}{\partial x}dx + \frac{\partial v}{\partial y}dy\right)}{dx + i\,dy} = \frac{\frac{\partial u}{\partial x} + i\frac{\partial v}{\partial x} + \left(\frac{\partial u}{\partial y} + i\frac{\partial v}{\partial y}\right)\frac{dy}{dx}}{1 + i\frac{dy}{dx}}.$$

The ratio of the differentials of w and z accordingly depends in general on the ratio of dy to dx, that is, if x and y represent the coordinates of a point in a plane, on the direction of leaving the point. If the ratio of dw to dz is to be independent of this direction and to depend only on the position of the point x, y, the numerator must be a multiple of the denominator, so that the expression containing $\frac{dy}{dx}$ divides out. In order that this may be true we must have

$$\left(\frac{\partial u}{\partial x} + i\frac{\partial v}{\partial x}\right) : 1 = \left(\frac{\partial u}{\partial y} + i\frac{\partial v}{\partial y}\right) : i,$$

that is

117) $$i\left(\frac{\partial u}{\partial x} + i\frac{\partial v}{\partial x}\right) = \frac{\partial u}{\partial y} + i\frac{\partial v}{\partial y}.$$

Putting real and imaginary parts on both sides equal,

118) $$\frac{\partial u}{\partial x} = \frac{\partial v}{\partial y}, \quad \frac{\partial v}{\partial x} = -\frac{\partial u}{\partial y},$$

and

119) $$\frac{dw}{dz} = \frac{\partial u}{\partial x} + i\frac{\partial v}{\partial x} = \frac{\partial v}{\partial y} - i\frac{\partial u}{\partial y}.$$

In this case the function w is said to have a definite derivative defined by

$$f'(z) = \lim_{\substack{dx=0 \\ dy=0}} \frac{dw}{dz},$$

and it is only when the functions u and v satisfy these conditions 118) that $u + iv$ is said to be an *analytic function* of z. This is Riemann's definition of a function of a complex variable.[1]) The real functions u and v are said to be *conjugate* functions of the real variables x, y.

It is obvious that if w is given as an analytic expression involving z, $w = f(z)$, then w always satisfies this condition. For

$$\frac{\partial w}{\partial x} = \frac{d f(z)}{dz}\frac{\partial z}{\partial x} = f'(z), \quad \frac{\partial w}{\partial y} = \frac{d f(z)}{dz}\frac{\partial z}{\partial y} = i f'(z).$$

Accordingly

$$i\frac{\partial w}{\partial x} = i\left(\frac{\partial u}{\partial x} + i\frac{\partial v}{\partial x}\right) = \frac{\partial w}{\partial y} = \frac{\partial u}{\partial y} + i\frac{\partial v}{\partial y},$$

$$\frac{\partial u}{\partial x} = \frac{\partial v}{\partial y}, \quad -\frac{\partial v}{\partial x} = \frac{\partial u}{\partial y}.$$

If we differentiate the equations 118), the first by x, and the second by y and add, since

$$\frac{\partial^2 v}{\partial x\,\partial y} = \frac{\partial^2 v}{\partial y\,\partial x},$$

we obtain

120) $$\frac{\partial^2 u}{\partial x^2} + \frac{\partial^2 u}{\partial y^2} = 0.$$

Differentiating the second by x and the first by y and subtracting, we find that v satisfies the same equation

121) $$\frac{\partial^2 v}{\partial x^2} + \frac{\partial^2 v}{\partial y^2} = 0.$$

Thus every function of a complex variable gives a pair of solutions of Laplace's equation, either one of which may be taken for the velocity potential, representing two different states of flow.

It is to be noticed that the question here dealt with is simply one of kinematics, since Laplace's equation is simply the equation of continuity and there is no reference to the dynamical equations.

The question arises whether any two solutions of Laplace's equation will conversely give us the function of a complex variable. It obviously will not answer to take *any* two harmonic functions, for they must be related so as to satisfy the equations 118) or be mutually conjugate. In order to avoid confusion with the velocity

1) Riemann, *Mathematische Werke*, p. 5.

components u and v, let us call the two conjugate functions φ and ψ, satisfying the equations

$$122)\qquad \frac{\partial \varphi}{\partial x} = \frac{\partial \psi}{\partial y}, \quad \frac{\partial \varphi}{\partial y} = -\frac{\partial \psi}{\partial x}.$$

It is evident that φ and ψ have the relation of the velocity potential and stream function defined in § 195. If one function is given we can find the conjugate, for we must have

$$d\psi = \frac{\partial \psi}{\partial x} dx + \frac{\partial \psi}{\partial y} dy,$$

which by equations 122) is

$$d\psi = -\frac{\partial \varphi}{\partial y} dx + \frac{\partial \varphi}{\partial x} dy.$$

Now if we call this $X dx + Y dy$ it satisfies the condition for a perfect differential

$$\frac{\partial X}{\partial y} = \frac{\partial Y}{\partial x}$$

that is, in this case,

$$-\frac{\partial^2 \varphi}{\partial y^2} = \frac{\partial^2 \varphi}{\partial x^2}.$$

Consequently the line integral

$$\int \left\{ -\frac{\partial \varphi}{\partial y} dx + \frac{\partial \varphi}{\partial x} dy \right\}$$

from a given point x_0, y_0 to a variable point x, y, is a function only of its upper limit and represents ψ. Similarly if ψ is given

$$123)\qquad \varphi = \int \left\{ \frac{\partial \varphi}{\partial x} dx + \frac{\partial \varphi}{\partial y} dy \right\} = \int \left\{ \frac{\partial \psi}{\partial y} dx - \frac{\partial \psi}{\partial x} dy \right\}.$$

Furthermore the first of the equations 122) is the condition that $\psi\, dx + \varphi\, dy$ is a perfect differential and the second that $\varphi\, dx - \psi\, dy$ is such. Accordingly the line integrals

$$124)\qquad \begin{aligned} \Phi &= \int \{\psi\, dx + \varphi\, dy\}, \\ \Psi &= \int \{\varphi\, dx - \psi\, dy\}, \end{aligned}$$

give two new point functions Φ, Ψ which in virtue of the equations

$$125)\qquad \begin{aligned} \psi &= \frac{\partial \Phi}{\partial x} = -\frac{\partial \Psi}{\partial y}, \\ \varphi &= \frac{\partial \Phi}{\partial y} = \frac{\partial \Psi}{\partial x}, \end{aligned}$$

are conjugate to each other and give a new analytic function of z,

$$(\Psi + i\Phi),$$

whose derivative is $\varphi + i\psi$. From these by new integrations we may obtain any number. The method of the complex variable accordingly gives us the solution of an unlimited number of uniplanar problems.

The equations 122) are geometrically the condition that the lines $\varphi = const.$, $\psi = const.$ intersect each other everywhere at right angles. If ψ is the stream function the lines $\psi = const.$ are the lines of flow, which we know intersect the equipotential surfaces at right angles. As examples consider the cases worked above,

$$w = z^2, \quad \varphi = x^2 - y^2, \quad \psi = 2xy.$$

The equipotential lines are sets of equilateral hyperbolas, intersected at right angles by the system of equilateral hyperbolas forming the stream lines (Fig. 164). The stream line $\psi = 0$ consists of the X and Y axes, which may accordingly be a boundary, so that one quarter

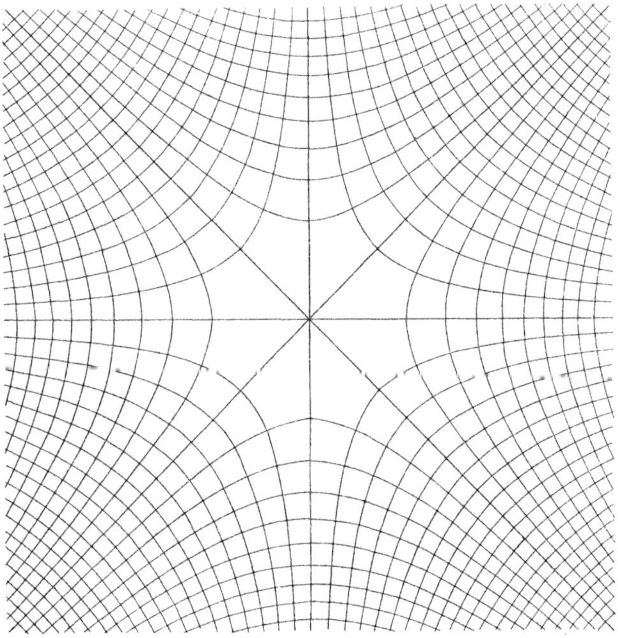

Fig. 164.

of the figure represents the flow in a square corner of a stream of infinite extent.

The function $w = \frac{1}{z}$ gives

$$\varphi = \frac{x}{x^2 + y^2}, \quad \psi = -\frac{y}{x^2 + y^2}.$$

The equipotential lines give a set of circles all tangent to the Y-axis at the origin, while the lines of flow are a similar set all tangent to the X-axis (Fig. 165). The water flows in on one side of the

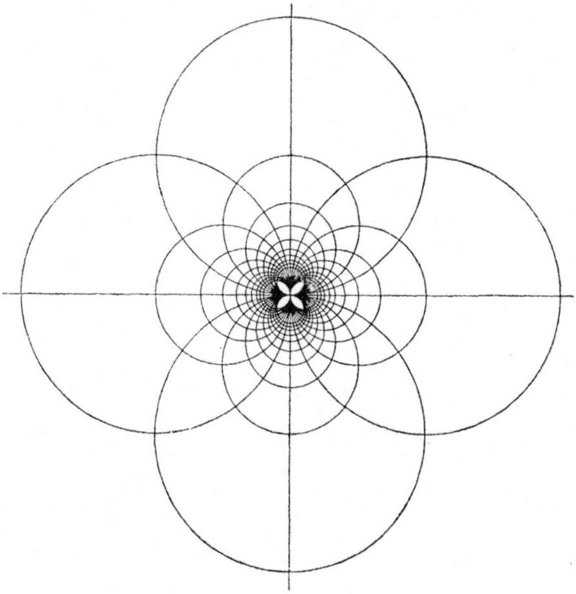

Fig. 165.

origin and out at the other as if there were a source on one side and an equal sink on the other close together.

The function z^n, of which the two examples just treated are particular cases, gives an interesting case which is most simply worked out by the introduction of polar coordinates.

$$x = r\cos\omega, \quad y = r\sin\omega,$$
$$z = x + iy = r(\cos\omega + i\sin\omega) = re^{i\omega},$$
$$z^n = r^n e^{in\omega} = r^n(\cos n\omega + i\sin n\omega),$$

from which we obtain the two conjugate functions

126) $$u = r^n\cos n\omega, \quad v = r^n\sin n\omega.$$

If we multiply these two harmonic functions by constants and add, the sum

127) $$r^n[A_n\cos(n\omega) + B_n\sin n\omega]$$

is the circular harmonic function treated in § 140. We may accordingly develop the velocity potential in a series of circular harmonics,

$$128)\qquad \varphi = \sum_n r^n \{A_n \cos n\omega + B_n \sin n\omega\},$$

and if we know the values of φ on the circumference of a circle with center at the origin, we may find the coefficients by the method of Fourier as in § 140a, 83).

Let us examine the motion in a segment between two walls making an angle 2α at the origin and reaching to infinity. If we use the value of φ given by equation 128), the coefficients and the values of n admissible are to be determined by the condition

$$\frac{\partial \varphi}{\partial n} = 0$$

along each wall. But since $dn = r\,d\omega$, we have

$$129)\qquad \frac{1}{r}\frac{\partial \varphi}{\partial \omega} = \sum_n n r^{n-1} \{B_n \cos n\omega - A_n \sin n\omega\}$$

which must vanish for $\omega = \pm\alpha$. If

$$n\alpha = \frac{2\varkappa + 1}{2}\pi, \quad \cos n\alpha = 0,$$

and if

$$n\alpha = \varkappa\pi, \quad \sin(\pm n\alpha) = 0,$$

$\varkappa$ being any integer. Therefore if we put when n is an odd multiple of $\frac{\pi}{2\alpha}$, $A_n = 0$ and $B_n = C_{2\varkappa+1}$ and for even multiples, $B_n = 0$ and $A_n = C_{2\varkappa}$, we shall have as a solution of the problem

$$130)\quad \varphi = \sum_\varkappa \left[C_{2\varkappa+1} r^{\frac{2\varkappa+1}{2}\frac{\pi}{\alpha}} \sin\left(\frac{2\varkappa+1}{2}\cdot\frac{\pi}{\alpha}\cdot\omega\right) + C_{2\varkappa} r^{\frac{\varkappa\pi}{\alpha}} \cos\left(\frac{\varkappa\pi}{\alpha}\omega\right) \right].$$

The tangential velocity at the wall is given by

$$131)\qquad \left(\frac{\partial \varphi}{\partial r}\right)_{\omega=\alpha} = \left[C_1 \frac{\pi}{2\alpha} r^{\frac{\pi}{2\alpha}-1} \sin\frac{\pi}{2} + \cdots \right].$$

The exponent of the lowest power of r is $\frac{\pi}{2\alpha} - 1$. If this is negative, that is if $\alpha > \frac{\pi}{2}$, the velocity is infinite for $r = 0$, that is at the corner, unless $C_1 = 0$.

The pressure is given by the equation

$$p = const. - \frac{\varrho}{2} q^2,$$

so that at a sharp projecting edge around which the water flows there would be an infinite negative pressure. This being impossible, around such an edge the motion is discontinuous, so that instead of

flowing as in a) Fig. 166, the water flows as in b), the flow being discontinuous at the dotted line. In actual fluids such surfaces of discontinuity give rise to vortex motion, so that we see eddies formed at projecting corners.

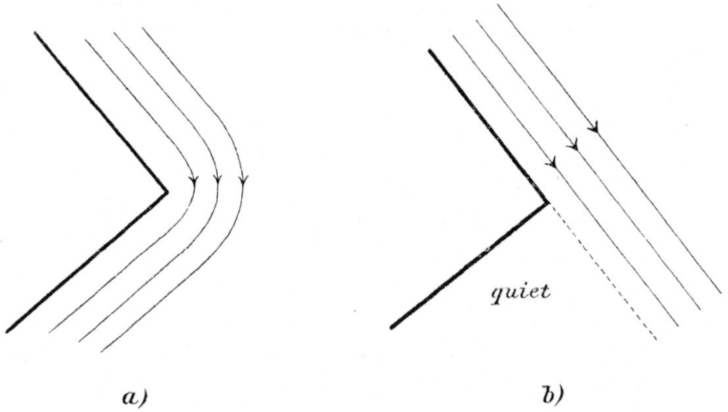

Fig. 166.

The function

$$\log z = \log r + i\omega$$

with

$$\varphi = \log r, \quad \psi = \omega,$$

gives us radial stream lines forming a uniplanar squirt, while

$$\varphi = \omega, \quad \psi = \log r$$

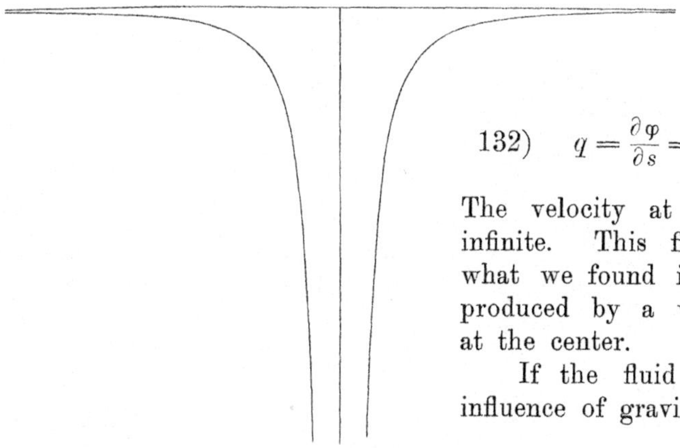

Fig. 167.

gives us flow in circles with a velocity

132) $$q = \frac{\partial \varphi}{\partial s} = \frac{1}{r}\frac{\partial \varphi}{\partial \omega} = \frac{1}{r}.$$

The velocity at the center is infinite. This flow is exactly what we found in § 195 to be produced by a vortex filament at the center.

If the fluid is under the influence of gravity, we have

42) $$p = const. - g\varrho z - \frac{1}{2}\varrho q^2$$

and for a free surface, $p = 0$,

133) $$C - g\varrho z - \frac{1}{2}\frac{\varrho}{r^2} = 0.$$

If z is zero when $r = \infty$, $C = 0$, and the equation of the surface is

$$- 2gz = \frac{1}{r^2}.$$

The form of the surface is shown in Fig. 167. This is approximately the form taken by the water running out of a circular orifice in the bottom of a tank, although the above investigation takes no account of the vertical motion.

198. Wave Motion. The case of uniplanar water waves may be dealt with by the method of the preceding section.[1] Let us take the XY-plane vertical, the Y-axis pointing vertically upward and the motion as before independent of the z coordinate, so that we may use z to denote the complex variable. We shall find that the waves travel with a constant velocity and it will therefore simplify the problem if we impress upon the whole mass of liquid an equal and opposite velocity so that the waves stand still and the motion is *steady*. Such still waves are actually seen on the surface of a running stream.

Let us first consider waves in very deep water. At a great depth the vertical motion will disappear and we shall have only the constant horizontal velocity that we have impressed, so that

$$u = - a, \quad v = 0,$$

from which

$$\varphi = - ax.$$

The function

$$f(z) = - az + Ae^{-ikz} = - a(x + iy) + Ae^{-ik(x+iy)}$$

gives

$$\varphi + i\psi = - a(x + iy) + Ae^{ky}(\cos kx - i \sin kx),$$

134)
$$\varphi = - ax + Ae^{ky} \cos kx,$$
$$\psi = - ay - Ae^{ky} \sin kx.$$

When $y = - \infty$ this makes $\varphi = - ax$, as required. The free surface of the water being composed of stream lines is represented by one of the lines $\psi = const.$ and if we take the origin in the surface its equation is consequently

135)
$$ay + Ae^{ky} \sin kx = 0,$$

which shows that y is a periodic function of x with the wave-length $\lambda = \frac{2\pi}{k}$. The longer the wave-length, that is the smaller k, the more

1) Rayleigh, *On Waves.* Phil. Mag. I, pp. 257—279, 1876. Scientific Papers, Vol. I, p. 261.

nearly does the exponential reduce to unity and the more nearly is the profile a curve of sines. The velocity is given by

136) $$q^2 = u^2 + v^2,$$

where

137) $$u = \frac{\partial \varphi}{\partial x} = \frac{\partial \psi}{\partial y} = -a - Ake^{ky} \sin kx,$$
$$v = \frac{\partial \varphi}{\partial y} = -\frac{\partial \psi}{\partial x} = Ake^{ky} \cos kx,$$

138) $$q^2 = a^2 + A^2k^2e^{2ky} + 2Aake^{ky} \sin kx.$$

So far all our work has been kinematical. The relation to dynamics is given by introducing the equation 33) for steady motion,

139) $$\frac{p}{\varrho} + gy + \frac{1}{2} q^2 = C,$$

and at the surface putting $p=0$, and making use of the equation 135),

140) $$gy + \frac{1}{2}\{a^2 + A^2k^2e^{2ky} - 2a^2ky\} = C.$$

Since the surface passes through the origin, putting $y = 0$ we obtain

$$C = \frac{1}{2}\{a^2 + A^2k^2\},$$

inserting which gives

141) $$(g - a^2k)y + \frac{1}{2}A^2k^2(e^{2ky} - 1) = 0.$$

This equation can be only approximately fulfilled, but if the height of the waves is small compared with the wave-length, so that $2ky$ is small, developing the exponential and neglecting terms of higher order than the first in ky we have

$$(g - a^2k + A^2k^3)\, y = 0,$$

giving the equation connecting the velocity and wave-length

142) $$g - a^2k + A^2k^3 = 0.$$

If ky is small the equation of the surface 135) is approximately

143) $$y = -\frac{A}{a} \sin kx$$

so that the maximum height of the waves above the origin is $B = \frac{A}{a}$. Inserting the values of the height and wave-length in equation 142) it becomes

144) $$a^2 \left\{\frac{2\pi}{\lambda}\left(1 - \frac{4\pi^2B^2}{\lambda^2}\right)\right\} = g,$$

an equation connecting the wave-length, height and velocity. For

waves long enough in comparison with their height to neglect $\frac{4\pi^2 B^2}{\lambda^2}$, we have

145) $$a^2 = \frac{g\lambda}{2\pi}.$$

If s is the height from which a body must fall to acquire a velocity equal to the wave-velocity, since $a^2 = 2gs$, the equation becomes

146) $$\lambda = 4\pi s,$$

accordingly the velocity of propagation of long waves in deep water is equal to the velocity acquired by a body falling freely from a height equal to one-half the radius of a circle whose circumference is the wave-length.

In order to study the motions of individual particles of water let us now impress upon the motion given by 137) a uniform velocity a in the X-direction. Equations 137) now give the motion with respect to moving axes travelling with the waves, so that in order to obtain the motion with respect to fixed axes we have to add a to the u of 137) and replace x by $x - at$, obtaining

147) $$\begin{aligned} u &= -Ake^{ky}\sin k(x - at), \\ v &= Ake^{ky}\cos k(x - at), \end{aligned}$$

for the equations of the unsteady motion of the actual wave-propagation. For the velocity of a particle we have

148) $$q = \sqrt{u^2 + v^2} = Ake^{ky}$$

showing that the velocity decreases rapidly as we go below the surface, so that for every increase of depth of one wave-length it is reduced in the ratio $e^{-2\pi} = .001867$. If the displacement of a particle which when at rest was at x, y is ξ, η we have

149) $$\begin{aligned} \frac{d\xi}{dt} &= -Ake^{ky}\sin k(x - at), \\ \frac{dy}{dt} &= Ake^{ky}\cos k(x - at), \end{aligned}$$

if we neglect the small change of velocity from x, y to $x + \xi, y + \eta$, so that we obtain by integration

150) $$\begin{aligned} \xi &= -Be^{ky}\cos k(x - at), \\ \eta &= -Be^{ky}\sin k(x - at). \end{aligned}$$

Thus each particle performs a uniform revolution in a circle of radius Be^{ky} in the periodic time $\frac{2\pi}{ka} = \frac{\lambda}{a}$. We thus see how the motion is confined to the surface layers. The direction of the motion in the orbit is such that particles at the crest of the wave move in the direction of the wave-propagation, those at a trough in the opposite direction.

Let us now discuss the form of the wave-profile 135) when the restriction that the height of the waves is small in comparison with the wave-length is removed. The equation of the surface is

151) $$y + Be^{ky} \sin kx = 0.$$

This may be conveniently done by means of a graphical construction, Fig. 168. Let us construct two curves, with the running coordinates X, Y, the first the logarithmic curve

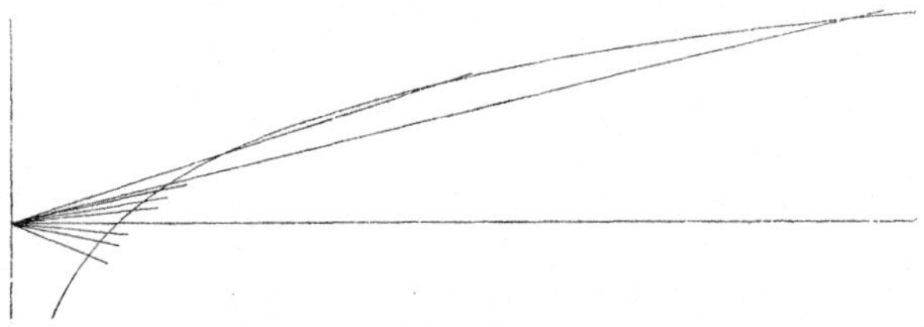

Fig. 168.

$$X = e^{kY}$$

and the second the straight line $X = -\frac{Y}{B \sin kx}$, which must be separately constructed for each value of x. At the intersection of the line and curve, we have

$$Y + Be^{kY} \sin kx = 0,$$

so that the value of Y thus obtained may be taken for the y coordinate of the wave-profile with the abscissa x. As x varies, the line swings back and forth about the X-axis, and we see that when $\sin kx$ is positive there is one intersection of the line and curve, while if $\sin kx$ is negative there are two, giving two values of y, both positive. Any positive y is greater in absolute value than the corresponding negative for the symmetrical position of the line. Thus the unsymmetrical nature of trough and crest is made evident. Beginning with $x = 0$, the two values of y are one zero, the other

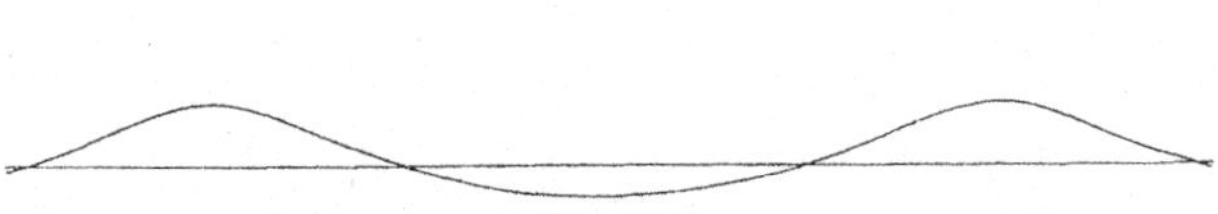

Fig. 169.

infinity, and as x increases, y has a single negative value. When $x = \frac{\pi}{k} = \frac{\lambda}{2}$, y is again zero and infinity, and as x increases the two values of y, both positive approach each other until $y = \frac{3}{4}\lambda$, then recede until $y = \lambda$. The form of the curve as constructed in this manner is shown in Fig. 169, the lower branch representing the wave-profile. If B is greater than a certain quantity the values of y between certain limits

are imaginary. This limiting value of B is that which makes the highest position of the straight line, for which $\sin kx = -1$, tangent to the exponential curve. We then have

$$\frac{dX}{dY} = kX \text{ for the curve, equal to } \frac{X}{Y} = \frac{1}{B} \text{ for the line,}$$

from which

$$kY = 1 = ky, \quad \frac{1}{B} = ke.$$

The upper and lower branches of the curve 151) then come together, and the wave-profile has an angle. Waves cannot be higher than this without breaking. By differentiation of 151) we find for the summit, $\frac{dy}{dx} = \pm 1$, so that the angle between the two sides of the wave is a right angle (Fig. 170). As a matter of fact, before the waves are as high as this, the equation 141) is no longer satisfied with sufficient approximation for the waves to have the form in question. By an elaborate system of approximation, Michell[1]) has shown that the highest waves have a height $.142\lambda$, while the equation 151) gives $.203\lambda$. It was shown by Stokes[2]) that at the crest the angle was not 90^0, but 120^0, as follows.

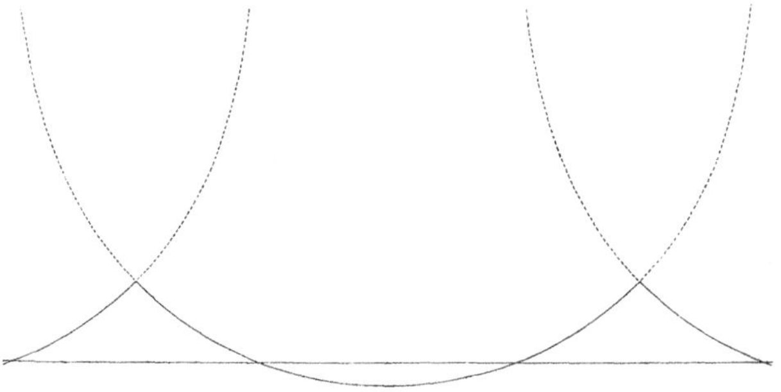

Fig. 170.

In the stationary wave, in order to have an edge, the velocities u and v for a particle at the surface must both vanish together, for if v alone vanishes, there will be a horizontal tangent. Consequently, if we place the origin at the crest, equation 139) becomes

$$gy + \frac{1}{2}q^2 = 0.$$

But if we represent the surface by a development of the form of equation 128), on account of symmetry there will be only sine terms, and if in the neighborhood of the origin we retain only the most important term, we may put

1) Michell, *The highest Waves in Water*. Phil. Mag. 36, p. 430, 1893.

2) Stokes, *On the Theory of Oscillatory Waves*. Trans. Cambridge Philosophical Society, Vol. VIII, p. 441, 1847. Math. and Phys. Papers, Vol. I, p. 227.

152) $$\varphi = Ar^n \sin n\omega, \quad \psi = Ar^n \cos n\omega,$$

ω being the angle measured from the vertical. We have for the radial velocity

$$q_r = \frac{\partial \varphi}{\partial r} = Anr^{n-1} \sin n\omega,$$

and if α is the inclination of the surface to the vertical at the crest $q = Anr^{n-1} \sin n\alpha$. But we have $q^2 = -2gy = 2gr\cos\alpha$ and accordingly $2(n-1) = 1$, $n = \frac{3}{2}$. Also as in 129), $\cos n\alpha = 0$. Thus

$$\frac{3}{2}\alpha = \frac{\pi}{2}, \quad 2\alpha = \frac{2\pi}{3} = 120^0.$$

The problem of waves in water of finite depth may be treated in a similar manner, by putting instead of 134),

$$\varphi + i\psi = -az + Ae^{-ikz} + Be^{ikz},$$

153)
$$\begin{aligned} \varphi &= -ax + (Ae^{ky} + Be^{-ky})\cos kx, \\ \psi &= -ay - (Ae^{ky} - Be^{-ky})\sin kx, \\ u &= -a - k(Ae^{ky} + Be^{-ky})\sin kx, \\ v &= k(Ae^{ky} - Be^{-ky})\cos kx. \end{aligned}$$

If the depth is h, we must have $v = 0$ for $y = -h$, giving

$$Ae^{-kh} = Be^{kh}.$$

Calling this value C, we have

154) $$\psi = -ay - C\left(e^{k(h+y)} - e^{-k(h+y)}\right)\sin kx = 0,$$

as the equation for the wave-profile. For the first approximation, for waves whose height is small compared to their length, replacing e^{ky}, e^{-ky} by unity, we have

155) $$ay = -C\left(e^{kh} - e^{-kh}\right) \cdot \sin kx,$$

and neglecting $(Ck)^2$,

156) $$u^2 + v^2 = a^2 + 2Cak\left(e^{kh} + e^{-kh}\right)\sin kx.$$

Thus the surface equation 139) becomes

157) $$const. = \frac{p}{\varrho} - \frac{Cg}{a}\left(e^{kh} - e^{-kh}\right)\sin kx + \frac{1}{2}\left[a^2 + 2Cak\left(e^{kh} + e^{-kh}\right)\sin kx\right],$$

which is satisfied by

158) $$ak\left(e^{kh} + e^{-kh}\right) - \frac{g}{a}\left(e^{kh} - e^{-kh}\right) = 0,$$

giving the velocity

159) $$a^2 = \frac{g}{k}\frac{e^{kh} - e^{-kh}}{e^{kh} + e^{-kh}}.$$

If h is infinite this reduces to 145), while if the depth is very small with respect to the wave-length, it reduces to $a^2 = gh$. Accordingly long waves in shallow water travel with a velocity independent of their length, being the velocity acquired by a body falling through a distance equal to one-half the depth of the water. Consequently the resultant of such waves of different wave-lengths is propagated without change, contrary to what is the case in deep water.

Changing to fixed axes, we have for the running wave

$$160)\quad \begin{aligned} \varphi &= \quad C\left(e^{k(h+y)} + e^{-k(h+y)}\right)\cos k\,(x - at),\\ \psi &= -C\left(e^{k(h+y)} - e^{-k(h+y)}\right)\sin k\,(x - at),\end{aligned}$$

and by comparison with 147), 150), we find that the particles describe ellipses with semi-axes equal to

$$161)\qquad \frac{C}{a}\left(e^{k(h+y)} + e^{-k(h+y)}\right),\quad \frac{C}{a}\left(e^{k(h+y)} - e^{-k(h+y)}\right).$$

If we consider the resultant of two equal wave-trains running in opposite directions, we have

$$162)\quad \begin{aligned} \varphi &= \quad C\left(e^{k(h+y)} + e^{-k(h+y)}\right)\left[\cos k\,(x - at) + \cos k\,(x + at)\right]\\ &= \quad 2C\left(e^{k(h+y)} + e^{-k(h+y)}\right)\cos kx \cos kat,\\ \psi &= -\quad C\left(e^{k(h+y)} - e^{-k(h+y)}\right)\left[\sin k\,(x - at) + \sin k\,(x + at)\right]\\ &= -2C\left(e^{k(h+y)} - e^{-k(h+y)}\right)\sin kx \cos kat.\end{aligned}$$

The equation of the profile is now of the form, y is equal to a function of x multiplied by a function of t, so that the profile is always of the same shape, with a varying vertical scale. Such waves are called *standing* waves, and we see them in a chop sea. The difference between them and the stationary wave in a running stream, with which we began, is very marked, as here every point on the surface oscillates up and down, while there the water-profile was invariable both as to time and place.

199. Equilibrium Theory of the Tides. We shall now briefly consider some aspects of the phenomena of the tides, the general theory of which is far too complicated to be dealt with here. The earliest theory historically is that proposed by Newton, which supposes that the water covering the earth assumes, under the attraction of a disturbing body, the form that it would have if *at rest* under the action of the forces in question. This so-called equilibrium theory, which neglects the inertia of the water, belongs logically to the subject of hydrostatics, but will be now treated. If U denote the potential of gravity, including the centrifugal force, as in § 149, we have, as there, for the undisturbed surface of the ocean,

163) $$U(r_0, \psi, \varphi) = const.$$

r_0, ψ, φ, denoting the radius, latitude, and longitude. If V denote the potential of the disturbing body, we have according to the equilibrium theory, for the disturbed surface,

164) $$U(r, \psi, \varphi) + V = const.$$

and subtracting equation 163) from this, we have

165) $$U(r, \psi, \varphi) - U(r_0, \psi, \varphi) + V = const. = C.$$

But if we put $h = r - r_0$, h is the height of the tide, and being small with respect to the radius, we may put

166) $$U(r, \psi, \varphi) - U(r_0, \psi, \varphi) = h\frac{\partial U}{\partial r},$$

giving

167) $$V - C = -h\frac{\partial U}{\partial r}.$$

But $g = -\gamma\frac{\partial U}{\partial r}$, as in § 149, so that we obtain for the height of the tide

168) $$h = \gamma\frac{V - C}{g}.$$

We may determine the constant in 168) by the consideration that the total volume of the water is constant. If dS is the area of an element of the earth's surface, the total volume of the tide above the surface of equilibrium must vanish, giving

169) $$0 = \iint h\,dS, \quad \iint V\,dS = C\iint dS, \quad \overline{V} = C,$$

where $\overline{V}$ is the mean value of the disturbing potential over the earth's surface. Now we have found in § 150, equation 154), the value of the potential of the tide-generating forces,

170) $$V = \frac{mr^2}{2D^3}(3\cos^2 Z - 1),$$

where Z is the zenith-distance of the heavenly body at the point in question. If we refer other points on the earth's surface to polar coordinates with respect to this point and any plane through it, with coordinates Z, Φ, we have

$$dS = r^2 \sin Z\,dZ\,d\Phi,$$

$$\iint V\,dS = \frac{mr^4}{2D^3}\int_0^{2\pi} d\Phi \int_0^{\pi} (3\cos^2 Z - 1)\sin Z\,dZ = 0,$$

so that the mean of V vanishes. Accordingly we have

171) $$h = \frac{\gamma m r^2}{2gD^3}(3\cos^2 Z - 1).$$

This equation shows that the tidal surface is a prolate ellipsoid of revolution, with its axis pointing at the disturbing body.

Let us now express $\cos Z$ in terms of the latitude ψ of the point of observation and of the declination δ and hour-angle H of the disturbing body, which for brevity we shall call the moon. If we take axes in the earth as usual, with the XZ-plane passing through the point of observation and measure H from this plane, we have for its coordinates and those of the moon respectively

$$\begin{array}{ll} r\cos\psi, & D\cos\delta\cos H, \\ 0\quad, & D\cos\delta\sin H, \\ r\sin\psi, & D\sin\delta\quad, \end{array}$$

from which we obtain the cosine of the angle included by their radii

$$\cos Z = \cos\psi\cos\delta\cos H + \sin\psi\sin\delta.$$

Squaring this, replacing $\cos^2 H$ by $\frac{1}{2}(1+\cos 2H)$, $\cos^2\psi\cos^2\delta$ by $(1-\sin^2\psi)(1-\sin^2\delta)$, we easily obtain

$$3\cos^2 Z - 1 = \frac{3}{2}\left[\cos^2\delta\cos^2\psi\cos 2H + \sin 2\delta\sin 2\psi\cos H + \frac{(1-3\sin^2\delta)(1-3\sin^2\psi)}{3}\right].$$

Inserting this in 171), replacing g by its approximate value $\frac{\gamma M}{r^2}$ and, as we have already done, neglecting the attraction of the disturbed water, we have the equation for the tide,

$$172)\quad \frac{h}{r} = \frac{3mr^3}{4MD^3}\left[\cos^2\delta\cos^2\psi\cos 2H + \sin 2\delta\sin 2\psi\cos H + \frac{(1-3\sin^2\delta)(1-3\sin^2\psi)}{3}\right].$$

The first term in the brackets, containing the factor $\cos 2H$, where H is the moon's hour-angle at the point of the earth in question, is periodic in one-half a lunar day, consequently this term has a maximum when the moon is on the meridian, both above and below, low water when the moon is rising or setting. The effect of this term is the semi-diurnal tide, which is the most familiar, with two high and two low waters each day. This tide is a maximum for points on the equator, where $\cos^2\psi = 1$, and for those times of the month when $\cos^2\delta = 1$, that is when the moon is crossing the equator. These are the so-called equinoctial tides.

The second term, containing the factor $\cos H$, is periodic in a lunar day, and gives the diurnal tide. This gives high water under the moon, and low water on the opposite side of the earth. On the side toward the moon, these two tides are therefore added, while on

the opposite side we have their difference. Consequently, at any point, the difference of two consecutive high waters is twice the diurnal tide. This difference is generally small, showing that the latter tide is small. It vanishes for points on the equator, and at the times of the equinoctial tides.

The third term, which vanishes for latitude $35^0\,16'$, does not depend on the moon's hour-angle, but only on its declination. This declinational tide, depending on the square of $\sin\delta$, has a period of one-half a lunar month.

Beside the tides due to the moon, we must add those due to the sun, for which the factor outside the brackets in 172) is somewhat less than one-half that due to the moon. The highest tides therefore occur at those times in the month when the sun and the moon are on the meridian together, namely at new and full moon. These are known as spring-tides. The lowest occur when the moon is in quadrature with the sun, and the lunar and solar tides are in opposition. These are known as neap-tides, and occording to this theory would be only one-third the height of the spring-tides. The greatest spring-tides would be those in which the moon was on the equator, or the equinoctial spring-tides. Now it is found that, instead of this, the high tides come about a day and a half later. Consequently, although the equilibrium theory indicates to us the general nature of the different tides to be expected, it does not give us an accurate expression for their values. Roughly speaking we may say that the tides act as if they were produced as described by the action of the sun and moon, but that the time of arrival of the effects produced was delayed.

A correction was introduced into the equilibrium theory by Lord Kelvin, to take account of the effect of the continents. For if the height of the tide were given by the equation 171), removing the various volumes of water in the space actually occupied by land would subtract an amount of water now positive, now negative, so that the condition of constant volume would not be fulfilled. In order that it still may do so, the integral 169) is to be taken only over those parts of the earth's surface covered by the sea. The value of $\overline{V}$ is then not zero. The effect of this is to introduce at each point on the earth's surface change of time of the arrival of each tide, varying from point to point. The practical effect of this correction is not large.

200. Tidal Waves in Canals. In the dynamical theory of the tides, taking account of the inertia of the water, we have the problem of the forced oscillations of the sea under periodic forces. As a simple example illustrating this method we shall consider waves

in straight canals. Let the motion be in the plane of XY, as in § 198, and let h, the depth of the canal, be small in comparison with the wave-length. We shall suppose the displacements of all the particles, with their velocities and their space-derivatives, to be small quantities whose squares and products may be neglected. We shall also neglect the vertical acceleration, so that the equation for y is that of hydrostatics, giving the pressure proportional to the distance below the surface. If the ordinate of the free surface is $h + \eta$, this gives

173) $$p = g\varrho(h + \eta - y),$$

174) $$\frac{\partial p}{\partial x} = g\varrho\frac{\partial \eta}{\partial x},$$

while the equation of motion, the first of equations 6), is

175) $$\frac{\partial u}{\partial t} = X - \frac{1}{\varrho}\frac{\partial p}{\partial x}.$$

Combining these two equations, we have

176) $$\frac{\partial u}{\partial t} = X - g\frac{\partial \eta}{\partial x},$$

and if X is independent of y, since $\frac{\partial \eta}{\partial x}$ is also, this shows that u depends only on x and t, or vertical planes perpendicular to the XY plane remain such during the motion.

Integrating the equation of continuity

$$\frac{\partial u}{\partial x} + \frac{\partial v}{\partial y} = 0,$$

with respect to y from the bottom to the surface,

177) $$v = -\int \frac{\partial u}{\partial x}dy = -(h + \eta)\frac{\partial u}{\partial x},$$

or approximately, at the surface,

178) $$v = \frac{\partial \eta}{\partial t} = -h\frac{\partial u}{\partial x}.$$

Now putting $u = \frac{\partial \xi}{\partial t}$, the equation of continuity 178) becomes,

179) $$\frac{\partial \eta}{\partial t} = -h\frac{\partial^2 \xi}{\partial t\,\partial x}$$

and on integration with respect to the time,

180) $$\eta = -h\frac{\partial \xi}{\partial x}.$$

Substituting in 176) we have for the horizontal displacement

181) $$\frac{\partial^2 \xi}{\partial t^2} = X + gh\frac{\partial^2 \xi}{\partial x^2}.$$

If there is no disturbing force, $X = 0$, and we have the equation

182) $$\frac{\partial^2 \xi}{\partial t^2} = gh \frac{\partial^2 \xi}{\partial x^2}$$

for the propagation of free waves, which we might have used in order to obtain the results of § 198, for instance it is satisfied by equations 150) if we put $a^2 = gh$. This is the same equation as we had in § 46, equation 109), for the motion of a stretched string, and the standing waves of 162), § 198, putting $y = 0$, are the normal vibrations of equation 115), § 46. The general solution of equation 182) is obtained in the next section, for the present it is sufficient to consider the wave already obtained which advances unchanged in form with the velocity a. We have then, in the case of an endless canal encircling the earth, the curvature of which we may neglect, the case of a free wave, running around and around, without change, so that at any point, the motion is periodic in the time $\frac{l}{a}$, where l is the length of the endless canal. We thus have a system with free periods, and when we consider the action upon it of periodic disturbing forces, we may expect the phenomena of resonance, as described in Chapter V.

Let us now suppose the canal coincides with a parallel of latitude, and that x is measured to the westward from a certain meridian. We then have for the horizontal component of the disturbing force

$$X = -\gamma \frac{\partial V}{\partial x}$$

where V is given by 170), and H, the hour-angle of the moon at the point x, is

183) $$H = \omega t - \frac{x}{r \cos \psi}, \quad \text{so that} \quad -\frac{\partial V}{\partial x} = \frac{\partial V}{\partial H} \frac{1}{r \cos \psi},$$

ω being the angular velocity of the moon with respect to the earth. We accordingly find X to be composed of two terms each of the form

$$-A \sin (mt - kx),$$

where for the semi-diurnal part

184) $$A = \frac{3}{2} \frac{\gamma m r}{D^3} \cos^2 \delta \cos \psi, \quad m = 2\omega, \quad k = \frac{2}{r \cos \psi} = \frac{4\pi}{l}.$$

Introducing this into the equation 181),

185) $$\frac{\partial^2 \xi}{\partial t^2} = a^2 \frac{\partial^2 \xi}{\partial x^2} - A \sin (mt - kx),$$

we may find a solution

186) $$\xi = B \sin(mt - kx),$$

where by insertion in 185) we find

187) $$B = \frac{A}{m^2 - a^2 k^2}.$$

From 180) we obtain

188) $$\eta = \frac{Akh}{a^2 k^2 - m^2} \cos(mt - kx).$$

The coefficient of the cosine is positive or negative according as ak is greater or less than m, so that we have, according to circumstances, high or low water under the moon. In the former case, the tides are said to be direct, as in the equilibrium theory, in the latter they are inverted. But $\frac{ka}{m}$ is the ratio of the time period of the force, or half a lunar day, to the time required for a free wave to travel half around the earth, and the tide is direct or inverted according as this is greater or less than unity. Equation 188) is the analogue of equation 50), § 44. Inserting the values of the constants in 188) we find that the canal theory gives the height of the tide as given by the equilibrium theory in 172) (which we also obtain by putting $m = 0$), multiplied by the factor

$$\frac{1}{1 - \left(\frac{m}{ak}\right)^2},$$

exactly as described for the system with one degree of freedom on page 155. If we introduced into our equations a term giving the effect of friction we should obtain a change of phase, as in § 44, of amount other than a half-period, or inversion.

In order to determine the directness or inversion of the tides, let us insert the values of m, k from 184) in 188), by which we find that the tides are direct or inverted according as we have the upper or lower sign in the inequality

189) $$gh \gtrless r^2 \omega^2 \cos^2 \psi.$$

Supposing the lunar day to be 24 hours, 50 minutes, the earth's circumference forty million meters, we find at the equator the critical depth, determining the inversion, to be 20.46 kilometers, or 12.7 miles. As the depth is less than this, the tides are inverted. For any depth less than the critical depth, there will be a latitude beyond which the tides will be direct. Accordingly we see that even if we consider the ocean to be composed of parallel canals separated by partitions, the tides will be very different in different latitudes, so that if the partitions be removed, water will flow north and south. We thus obtain an idea of the complication of the actual motion of the tides.

By introducing the complete expressions for the accelerations with respect to revolving axes, given in § 104, and applying the principles of forced oscillations, we obtain the more complete theory given by Laplace.

201. Sound-Waves. Let us now consider the motion of a compressible fluid which takes place in the propagation of sound. In the production of all ordinary sounds, except those violent ones produced by explosions, the motion of each particle of air is extremely minute. We shall therefore suppose that the velocity components u, v, w and their space derivatives are so small that their squares and products may be neglected. Let us put

190) $$\varrho = \varrho_0 (1 + s),$$

where ϱ_0 is a constant and s is a small quantity, of the same order as the velocities, called the compression. From the equation of continuity we have

191) $$\sigma = \frac{\partial u}{\partial x} + \frac{\partial v}{\partial y} + \frac{\partial w}{\partial z} = -\frac{1}{\varrho}\frac{\partial \varrho}{\partial t} = -\frac{1}{1+s}\frac{\partial s}{\partial t},$$

or neglecting the product of s and its derivative,

192) $$\sigma = -\frac{\partial s}{\partial t}.$$

In order to calculate P, we have, since the changes in ϱ are small

193) $$dp = a^2 d\varrho = a^2 \varrho_0 \, ds,$$

where a^2 is a constant representing the value of the derivative $\frac{dp}{d\varrho}$ for $\varrho = \varrho_0$, the density of the air at atmospheric pressure. We therefore have

194) $$P = \int \frac{dp}{\varrho} = \int \frac{a^2 ds}{1+s} = a^2 \log(1+s) = a^2 s,$$

to the same degree of approximation.

Neglecting small quantities the equations of hydrodynamics 6) become, when there are no applied forces,

195) $$\frac{\partial u}{\partial t} = -a^2 \frac{\partial s}{\partial x}, \quad \frac{\partial v}{\partial t} = -a^2 \frac{\partial s}{\partial y}, \quad \frac{\partial w}{\partial t} = -a^2 \frac{\partial s}{\partial z},$$

with

192) $$\sigma = -\frac{\partial s}{\partial t}.$$

Differentiating the equations respectively by x, y, z, adding and observing the definition of σ, we obtain

196) $$\frac{\partial \sigma}{\partial t} = - a^2 \Delta s,$$

and differentiating 192) by t and combining with this

197) $$\frac{\partial^2 s}{\partial t^2} = a^2 \Delta s.$$

Since the motion is assumed to be irrotational, introducing the velocity potential into equations 195) they become the derivatives by x, y, z respectively of the equation

198) $$\frac{\partial \varphi}{\partial t} = - a^2 s.$$

Differentiating by t, making use of equation 192),

199) $$\frac{\partial^2 \varphi}{\partial t^2} = - a^2 \frac{\partial s}{\partial t} = a^2 \sigma = a^2 \Delta \varphi.$$

Thus both the velocity potential and the compression satisfy the differential equation

200) $$\frac{\partial^2 \varphi}{\partial t^2} = a^2 \Delta \varphi.$$

This is known as the differential equation of wave-motion and is the basis of the theories of sound and light.

202. Plane Waves. Let us suppose first that the motion is the same at all points in each plane perpendicular to a given direction which we will take for that of the X-axis. Thus all the quantities concerned become independent of y and z and equation 200) reduces to

201) $$\frac{\partial^2 \varphi}{\partial t^2} = a^2 \frac{\partial^2 \varphi}{\partial x^2},$$

which is equation 109) § 46, the equation for the motion of a continuous string, or equation 182) § 200, for the propagation of long waves in shallow water.

The general solution of this equation is found by introducing the two new independent variables $p = x - at$, $q = x + at$.

We have then

202) $$\begin{aligned} \frac{\partial \varphi}{\partial t} &= \frac{\partial \varphi}{\partial p}\frac{\partial p}{\partial t} + \frac{\partial \varphi}{\partial q}\frac{\partial q}{\partial t} = - a\frac{\partial \varphi}{\partial p} + a\frac{\partial \varphi}{\partial q}, \\ \frac{\partial \varphi}{\partial x} &= \frac{\partial \varphi}{\partial p}\frac{\partial p}{\partial x} + \frac{\partial \varphi}{\partial q}\frac{\partial q}{\partial x} = \frac{\partial \varphi}{\partial p} + \frac{\partial \varphi}{\partial q}, \\ \frac{\partial^2 \varphi}{\partial t^2} &= a^2 \left\{ \frac{\partial^2 \varphi}{\partial p^2} + \frac{\partial^2 \varphi}{\partial q^2} - 2\frac{\partial^2 \varphi}{\partial p \partial q} \right\}, \\ \frac{\partial^2 \varphi}{\partial x^2} &= \frac{\partial^2 \varphi}{\partial p^2} + \frac{\partial^2 \varphi}{\partial q^2} + 2\frac{\partial^2 \varphi}{\partial p \partial q}. \end{aligned}$$

Inserting these values in 201), we have

203) $$\frac{\partial^2 \varphi}{\partial p \partial q} = 0.$$

Integrating with respect to q, we find that $\frac{\partial \varphi}{\partial p}$ is independent of q, but may be an arbitrary function of p, say

$$\frac{\partial \varphi}{\partial p} = F_1'(p).$$

Integrating again we find

204) $$\varphi = F_1(p) + F_2(q),$$

where F_2 is an arbitrary function of q. Whatever the functions F_1 and F_2, this value will satisfy the equation 203). Replacing p and q by their values, we have the general solution

205) $$\varphi = F_1(x - at) + F_2(x + at).$$

Let us first assume $F_2 = 0$ and consider the solution

206) $$\varphi = F_1(p) = F_1(x - at).$$

The value of φ depending only on p is unchanged when x has increased by the amount at, that is to say, if φ be represented graphically as a function of x at the time $t = 0$, it will be represented at the time t by the same curve moved to the right a distance at. Such a motion is termed a *wave* moving with the velocity a in the positive X-direction.

Similarly the solution

207) $$\varphi = F_2(q) = F_2(x + at)$$

represents a wave moving in the negative X-direction with the same velocity.

If the function $F(p)$ is zero except for a certain small range of values p_0, p_1, the motion is sometimes called a pulse. A pulse is none the less a wave.

Thus the general solution of equation 201) represents two plane waves propagated in opposite directions with the same velocity a.

The velocity of sound $a = \sqrt{\frac{dp}{d\varrho}}$ depends upon the elasticity of the air and was calculated by Newton, assuming that the process was isothermal, using Boyle's law. As this was found to give results not agreeing with experiment Laplace suggested that the compression was adiabatic, the vibrations being so rapid that the heat generated did not have time to flow from the heated to the cooled parts. Thus the constant $\varkappa$, equation 17) § 178 representing the ratio of the two specific heats of the air is introduced. The velocity of sound gives one of the most accurate ways of determining this ratio $\varkappa$.

The velocity of the particle of air is obtained by

208) $$u = \frac{\partial \varphi}{\partial x} = F_1'(x - at)$$

in the wave going to the right. The compression by

209) $$s = -\frac{1}{a^2}\frac{\partial \varphi}{\partial t} = \frac{1}{a} F_1'(x - at),$$

so that

$$u = as.$$

Thus the velocity of the particle is in the same direction as that of the wave where there is condensation, or s is positive, in the opposite direction where there is rarefaction, or s is negative.

203. Echo. Organ-pipes. Suppose there is a rigid wall whose equation is $x = l$. The velocity of a particle normal to the wall must be zero, so that

210) $$u = F_1'(x - at) + F_2'(x + at) = 0$$

when $x = l$, or

211) $$F_1'(l - at) + F_2'(l + at) = 0$$

for all positive values of t. Thus one of the functions is determined by the other. Put

$$l + at = y,$$

so that our equation 211) is

212) $$F_2'(y) = -F_1'(2l - y),$$

a differential equation connecting F_1 and F_2, the integral of which is

213) $$F_2(y) = F_1(2l - y) + C$$

for $y \geqq l$. Since the velocity depends only on the derivative of φ, the value of C is immaterial, and we will put it equal to zero.

The equation $F_2(y) = F_1(2l - y)$ indicates that the curve representing F_2 is the geometrical reflection in the wall of that representing F_1, in other words the function F_2 represents a wave travelling to the left, which after $x - at$ is greater than l represents the motion on the left of the wall, the values of φ at points a certain distance to the left of the wall being the same as they would have been at the same distance to the right of the wall had the direct wave gone on unchanged. Since the values of u depend on the derivative of φ according to x, the velocity changes sign in the reflection. This must be the case for the condition producing reflection is that $u = 0$ at $x = l$, so that the wave coning to the left must have a velocity equal and opposite to that of the wave going to the right. If there is a wall at $x = 0$ as well as at $x = l$, the wave is reflected in that also, so that the motion consists in the continual to and fro motion of the original disturbance. The motion at any point is periodic in the time $\frac{2l}{a}\cdot$ We may accordingly develop the motion

in a series of normal vibrations as in § 46. If we take the particular solution of equation 109) given in equation 115) of that section, and write

213) $$\varphi = A \cos kx \cos nt,$$

where $n = ka$, we have

214) $$u = \frac{\partial \varphi}{\partial x} = -Ak \sin kx \cos nt,$$
$$s = -\frac{1}{a^2}\frac{\partial \varphi}{\partial t} = A\frac{n}{a^2} \cos kx \sin nt.$$

Every particle oscillates with a simple harmonic motion with an amplitude $\frac{A}{a} \sin kx$, and we have a *pure tone*. The compression also varies harmonically with an amplitude $\frac{Ak}{a} \cos kx$. Thus the maximum pressure occurs at points of no motion, such points being called nodes. These occur where $kx = r\pi$, where r is any integer, or $x = \frac{\pi}{k}, \frac{2\pi}{k}, \frac{3\pi}{k}, \ldots$. The wave-length being $\lambda = \frac{2\pi}{k}$, the nodes are separated by distances $\frac{\lambda}{2}$. The condensation s follows a similar law, but vanishes half way between the nodes where the motion is a maximum. The regions between the nodes are called loops. The maximum changes of s are at the nodes.

As there is no motion at the nodes, but only changes of pressure, we may place reflecting walls there and apply the theory to the case of a stopped organ-pipe, whose length is accordingly any number of half wave-lengths. If the ends of the pipe are at $x = 0$ and $x = l$, we have

$$l = r\frac{\lambda}{2}, \quad kl = r\pi, \quad k = \frac{r\pi}{l},$$

and the frequency is determined by

$$\frac{n}{2\pi} = \frac{ak}{2\pi} = \frac{ar}{2l}.$$

Consequently the possible frequencies for a simple harmonic vibration of a stopped pipe are in the ratio of the integers 1, 2, 3, etc.

For a pipe open at the end the condition is that the pressure is that of the external air, that is, there is a loop. Thus a pipe open at both ends has its length equal to an integral number of half wave-lengths, and has the same harmonics as a closed pipe. Opening one of the holes in a flute produces a loop, so that the tones of a flute are produced by the column of air between the mouth-piece and the first open hole.

For a pipe open at one end and stopped at the other, the length is equal to an odd number of quarter wave-lengths, so that the frequencies are proportional to the odd integers 1, 3, 5, etc.

204. Spherical Waves. If the velocity potential depends only on the distance from a fixed point, using the expression of § 135, equation 44), the wave-equation 200) becomes

$$215)\qquad \frac{\partial^2 \varphi}{\partial t^2} = a^2 \left\{ \frac{\partial^2 \varphi}{\partial r^2} + \frac{2}{r}\frac{\partial \varphi}{\partial r} \right\} = \frac{a^2}{r}\frac{\partial^2 (r\varphi)}{\partial r^2}.$$

Multiplying by r, this is

$$216)\qquad \frac{\partial^2 (r\varphi)}{\partial t^2} = a^2 \frac{\partial^2 (r\varphi)}{\partial r^2},$$

so that the product $r\varphi$ satisfies an equation like 201), of which the solution is

$$r\varphi = F_1(r - at) + F_2(r + at).$$

Accordingly we have

$$217)\qquad \varphi = \frac{1}{r}\{F_1(r - at) + F_2(r + at)\},$$

of which the first term represents a wave proceeding outwards, the second one proceeding inwards, the magnitude however varying according to the factor $\frac{1}{r}$.

For a periodic solution representing a simple tone proceeding from a single point-source we may take

$$218)\qquad \varphi = -\frac{A}{4\pi r}\cos k(at - r).$$

The physical meaning of the constant A is obtained as follows. Let us find the volume of air flowing in unit of time through the surface of a sphere with center at the source. We will call this the total current,

$$219)\qquad I = \iint q\cos(qn)\,dS = \iint \frac{\partial \varphi}{\partial r}\,dS = 4\pi r^2 \frac{\partial \varphi}{\partial r}$$
$$= A\{\cos k(at - r) - kr\sin k(at - r)\}.$$

Accordingly when $r = 0$ we have $I = A\cos kat$ and A, the maximum rate of emission of air per unit of time, is called the *strength* of the source, agreeing with the definition of § 196.

In order to obtain the activity of the source, that is the rate of emission of energy per unit of time, we may find the rate of working of the pressure at the surface of a sphere, as explained in § 188,

$$220)\qquad P = \iint pq\,dS = 4\pi r^2 p \frac{\partial \varphi}{\partial r}.$$

In order to find p, we have, if p_0 is the undisturbed atmospheric pressure, by integration of 193), and by 198),

221) $$p - p_0 = a^2 \varrho_0 s = - \varrho_0 \frac{\partial \varphi}{\partial t}$$

from which we obtain

222) $$P = A\left\{\cos k(at-r) - kr \sin k(at-r)\right\}\left\{p_0 - \frac{A\varrho_0 k a}{4\pi r}\sin k(at-r)\right\}.$$

This contains a part which is alternately positive and negative, and also one which is always positive. If we seek the mean value of P throughout the period, that is

$$\bar{P} = \frac{1}{T}\int_0^T P\,dt, \quad T = \frac{2\pi}{ka},$$

we easily find, since the mean of $\cos\vartheta$, $\sin\vartheta$, $\cos\vartheta\sin\vartheta$, is zero, while the mean of $\sin^2\vartheta$ is $\frac{1}{2}$,

223) $$\bar{P} = \frac{A^2 \varrho_0 k^2 a}{8\pi}$$

which is independent of the radius, as it should be. The mean energy-flow per unit of time and per unit of area of the sphere is

224) $$\frac{\bar{P}}{S} = \frac{A\varrho_0 k^2 a}{32\pi^2 r^2}$$

which is a measure of the intensity of the sound. Tihs decreases as the inverse square of the distance. In order to give an idea of the extremely small dynamical magnitudes involved in musical sounds, it may be stated that measurements made by the author[1]) showed that the energy emitted by a cornet, playing with an average loudness, was 770 ergs per second, or about one ten-millionth of a horse-power, while a steam-whistle that could under favorable circumstances be heard twenty miles away emitted but $\frac{1.25 \times 10^2 \text{ ergs}}{\text{sec.}}$, or one-sixtieth of a horse-power (see note, p. 153).

205. Waves in a Solid. The equations of motion for an elastic solid are obtained from the equations of equilibrium 144), § 175 by the application of d'Alembert's principle in the same manner as the equations of hydrodynamics were deduced from those of hydrostatics. It will be convenient here to revert to the notation of Chapter IX where u, v, w and σ refer to displacements rather than to velocities. Applying d'Alembert's principle we thus obtain

225) $$\varrho\left(X - \frac{\partial^2 u}{\partial t^2}\right) + (\lambda + \mu)\frac{\partial \sigma}{\partial x} + \mu \Delta u = 0, \text{ etc.}$$

---

1) Webster, *On the Mechanical Efficiency of the Production of Sound.* Boltzmann-Festschrift, p. 866, 1904.

If there are no bodily forces we have the equations of motion

226)
$$\varrho \frac{\partial^2 u}{\partial t^2} = (\lambda + \mu)\frac{\partial \sigma}{\partial x} + \mu \Delta u,$$
$$\varrho \frac{\partial^2 v}{\partial t^2} = (\lambda + \mu)\frac{\partial \sigma}{\partial y} + \mu \Delta v,$$
$$\varrho \frac{\partial^2 w}{\partial t^2} = (\lambda + \mu)\frac{\partial \sigma}{\partial z} + \mu \Delta w.$$

Differentiating respectively by x, y, z and adding we obtain

227)
$$\varrho \frac{\partial^2 \sigma}{\partial t^2} = (\lambda + 2\mu)\Delta \sigma,$$

which is the equation for the propagation of wave-motion, the dilatation being propagated with a velocity $b = \sqrt{\frac{\lambda + 2\mu}{\varrho}}$. Taking the curl of equations 226) we have

228)
$$\varrho \frac{\partial^2 \xi}{\partial t^2} = \mu \Delta \xi,$$
$$\varrho \frac{\partial^2 \eta}{\partial t^2} = \mu \Delta \eta,$$
$$\varrho \frac{\partial^2 \zeta}{\partial t^2} = \mu \Delta \zeta.$$

Thus the components of the curl are propagated independently, each with a velocity $a = \sqrt{\frac{\mu}{\varrho}}$. The velocity of the compressional wave which is unaccompanied by rotation depends upon the bulk modulus and the modulus of shear. The velocity of the torsional wave which is unaccompanied by change of density depends only upon the modulus of shear. The general motion of an elastic body is a combination of waves of compression and of torsion. The wave of torsion is that upon which the dynamical theory of light is founded. Inasmuch as μ vanishes for a perfect fluid no wave of torsion is propagated, so that the luminiferous ether must have the properties of a solid and not those of a fluid.

206. Viscous Fluids. We have now to consider a class of bodies intermediate in their properties between solids and perfect fluids, namely the viscous fluids. By definition a perfect fluid is one in which no tangential stresses exist. We have then

229)
$$X_x = Y_y = Z_z = -p, \quad X_y = Y_z = Z_x = 0.$$

In a fluid which is not perfect no tangential stresses can exist in a state of rest, but during motion such stresses can exist. While in a solid the stresses depend on the change of size and shape of the small portions of the solid, in the case of a viscous fluid the stresses

depend on the time-rates of change, that is on the velocities of the shears, stretches, and dilatations. The simplest assumption that we can make is that the stress-components are linear functions of the strain-velocities. The fluid being isotropic, considerations regarding invariance bring us to precisely similar conclusions to those we reached in § 175, so that to the stresses of equations 229) for a perfect fluid are added stresses given by equations 142), § 175, λ and μ being constants for the fluid, and u, v, w, σ now denoting velocities, instead of displacements, returning to the notation of this chapter. (We put $P=0$, since these additional terms vanish with the velocities.) We thus obtain

230)
$$\begin{aligned} X_x &= -p + \lambda\sigma + 2\mu\frac{\partial u}{\partial x},\\ Y_y &= -p + \lambda\sigma + 2\mu\frac{\partial v}{\partial y},\\ Z_z &= -p + \lambda\sigma + 2\mu\frac{\partial w}{\partial z},\\ Y_z = Z_y &= \mu\left(\frac{\partial w}{\partial y} + \frac{\partial v}{\partial z}\right),\\ Z_x = X_z &= \mu\left(\frac{\partial u}{\partial z} + \frac{\partial w}{\partial x}\right),\\ X_y = Y_x &= \mu\left(\frac{\partial v}{\partial x} + \frac{\partial u}{\partial y}\right), \end{aligned}$$

which are of the same form, with a different meaning, as 142), § 175. If the fluid is incompressible we find, putting $\sigma = 0$,

$$X_x + Y_y + Z_z = -3p,$$

and assuming that this holds also for compressible fluids we must have

231)
$$3\lambda + 2\mu = 0.$$

Replacing λ by its value $-\frac{2}{3}\mu$, we find for the forces, as in § 175, 144),

232)
$$\begin{aligned} &\varrho X - \frac{\partial p}{\partial x} + \frac{1}{3}\mu\frac{\partial\sigma}{\partial x} + \mu\Delta u,\\ &\varrho Y - \frac{\partial p}{\partial y} + \frac{1}{3}\mu\frac{\partial\sigma}{\partial y} + \mu\Delta v,\\ &\varrho Z - \frac{\partial p}{\partial z} + \frac{1}{3}\mu\frac{\partial\sigma}{\partial z} + \mu\Delta w, \end{aligned}$$

which are to be introduced into the equations of hydrodynamics 6). Thus we obtain the general equations, putting $\frac{\mu}{\varrho} = \nu$,

233)
$$\begin{aligned} \frac{\partial u}{\partial t} + u\frac{\partial u}{\partial x} + v\frac{\partial u}{\partial y} + w\frac{\partial u}{\partial z} - \frac{\nu}{3}\frac{\partial\sigma}{\partial x} - \nu\Delta u &= X - \frac{1}{\varrho}\frac{\partial p}{\partial x},\\ \frac{\partial v}{\partial t} + u\frac{\partial v}{\partial x} + v\frac{\partial v}{\partial y} + w\frac{\partial v}{\partial z} - \frac{\nu}{3}\frac{\partial\sigma}{\partial y} - \nu\Delta v &= Y - \frac{1}{\varrho}\frac{\partial p}{\partial y},\\ \frac{\partial w}{\partial t} + u\frac{\partial w}{\partial x} + v\frac{\partial w}{\partial y} + w\frac{\partial w}{\partial z} - \frac{\nu}{3}\frac{\partial\sigma}{\partial z} - \nu\Delta w &= Z - \frac{1}{\varrho}\frac{\partial p}{\partial z}, \end{aligned}$$

which reduce to 6) when $\mu = 0$. The coefficient μ is called the viscosity of the fluid, and its quotient by the density, ν, is called by Maxwell the kinematical coefficient of viscosity.

The equations 233) are too complicated to be used in all their generality. We shall here consider only the case of incompressible fluids, for which the terms in σ vanish. If we form the equation of activity as in § 188, we obtain beside the terms in the first integral of 29) the additional terms

$$-\mu\iiint(u\Delta u + v\Delta v + w\Delta w)\,d\tau,$$

which by Green's theorem may be converted into

$$\iint\left(u\frac{\partial u}{\partial n} + v\frac{\partial v}{\partial n} + w\frac{\partial w}{\partial n}\right)dS$$
$$+\iiint\left\{\left(\frac{\partial u}{\partial x}\right)^2 + \left(\frac{\partial u}{\partial y}\right)^2 + \left(\frac{\partial u}{\partial z}\right)^2 + \left(\frac{\partial v}{\partial x}\right)^2 + \cdots\right\}d\tau.$$

If the integration be extended to a region where the liquid is at rest, say the surface of a containing solid, where the liquid does not slip, the surface integrals vanish, and the volume integrals give a *positive* addition. That is to say, the applied forces have to do an amount of work over and above that going into kinetic and potential energy, and this work is *dissipated* into heat. If there are no applied forces, the energy of the fluid is dissipated, and it will eventually come to rest.

In order to find simple solutions of our equations, we may deal either with steady motion, or with motions so slow that we may neglect the terms of the second order in u, v, w and their derivatives. Let us first consider steady motion. The simplest case is uniplanar flow parallel to a single direction, or as we may call it, *laminar* flow. If we take

234) $$0 = v = w = \frac{\partial u}{\partial z} = \frac{\partial p}{\partial z},$$

the equation of continuity gives

235) $$\frac{\partial u}{\partial x} = 0.$$

If there are no applied forces, equations 233) reduce to

236) $$\mu\frac{\partial^2 u}{\partial y^2} = \frac{\partial p}{\partial x}, \quad \frac{\partial p}{\partial y} = 0.$$

Since u depends only on y and p only on x, this equation cannot hold unless each side is constant. Accordingly

237) $$\mu\frac{d^2 u}{dy^2} = a = \frac{dp}{dx}, \quad u = c + by + \frac{1}{2}\frac{a}{\mu}y^2, \quad p = d + ax,$$

where a, b, c, d are constants. If we determine them so that the velocity vanishes for planes at a distance $\pm h$ from the X-axis, we have

$$238)\qquad u = \frac{a}{2\mu}(y^2 - h^2).$$

The amount of liquid that flows through such a laminar tube per unit of width parallel to the Z-axis is accordingly

$$239)\qquad Q = \int_{-h}^{h} u\,dy = -\frac{2}{3}\frac{ah^3}{\mu}$$

and for a length of tube l the difference of pressures at the ends is

$$240)\qquad p_2 - p_1 = al, \quad Q = \frac{2}{3}\frac{h^3}{\mu}\frac{(p_1 - p_2)}{l},$$

so that the flow is proportional to the difference of pressures at the ends and inversely to the viscosity.

For the practical determination of viscosity, we may take the almost equally simple case of cylindrical flow, where the velocity has everywhere the same direction, and depends upon the distance r from the axis of a circular tube, at the surface of which it is at rest.

If we put $u = v = 0$ we have the equations of motion and of continuity

$$241)\qquad \mu \Delta w = \frac{\partial p}{\partial z}, \quad \frac{\partial p}{\partial x} = \frac{\partial p}{\partial y} = 0, \quad \frac{\partial w}{\partial z} = 0,$$

and since w depends only on r the first becomes

$$242)\qquad \mu\left\{\frac{d^2 w}{dr^2} + \frac{1}{r}\frac{dw}{dz}\right\} = \frac{dp}{dz} = a,$$

where a is a constant as before. This equation is integrated as in § 182, 58'),

$$243)\qquad w = \frac{a}{4\mu} r^2 + b \log r + c.$$

Since w is finite when $r = 0$ we must have $b = 0$ and if w vanishes for $r = R$ we obtain

$$244)\qquad w = \frac{a}{4\mu}(r^2 - R^2).$$

For the flow we find

$$245)\qquad Q = \int_0^R 2\pi w r\,dr = \frac{a\pi R^4}{8\mu} = \frac{\pi R^4}{8\mu}\frac{(p_1 - p_2)}{l}.$$

This method was invented by Poiseuille[1]) for the measurement of

---

1) Poiseuille, *Recherches expérimentales sur le mouvement des liquides dans les tubes de très petits diamètres.* Comptes Rendus, 1840—41; Mém. des Savants Étrangers, t. 9, 1846.

the viscosity of fluids. His verification of the proportionality of the flow to the fourth power of the radius of the tube has been taken as a proof that the liquid does not slide when in contact with a solid.

As another example of steady flow let us consider uniplanar cylindrical flow, in which each particle moves in a circle with velocity depending only on the distance from the axis, as in the case of the lubricant between a journal and its bearing. Each cylindrical stratum then revolves like a rigid body, which requires

246) $$u = -\omega y, \quad v = \omega x,$$

where ω depends only on $r = \sqrt{x^2 + y^2}$. We then find

247) $$\frac{\partial u}{\partial x} = -\frac{xy}{r}\frac{d\omega}{dr}, \quad \frac{\partial u}{\partial y} = -\omega - \frac{y^2}{r}\frac{d\omega}{dr}, \qquad \frac{\partial v}{\partial x} = \omega + \frac{x^2}{r}\frac{d\omega}{dr}, \quad \frac{\partial v}{\partial y} = \frac{xy}{r}\frac{d\omega}{dr},$$

and, most easily by the application of equation 86), § 141, and by the expression of $\Delta\omega$ in terms of r,

248) $$\Delta u = -y\left(\frac{d^2\omega}{dr^2} + \frac{1}{r}\frac{d\omega}{dr}\right) - 2\frac{y}{r}\frac{d\omega}{dr}, \qquad \Delta v = x\left(\frac{d^2\omega}{dr^2} + \frac{1}{r}\frac{d\omega}{dr}\right) + 2\frac{x}{r}\frac{d\omega}{dr}.$$

Thus the first two of equations 233) become

249) $$-\omega^2 x + \nu y\left(\frac{d^2\omega}{dr^2} + \frac{3}{r}\frac{d\omega}{dr}\right) = -\frac{1}{\varrho}\frac{x}{r}\frac{dp}{dr}, \qquad -\omega^2 y - \nu x\left(\frac{d^2\omega}{dr^2} + \frac{3}{r}\frac{d\omega}{dr}\right) = -\frac{1}{\varrho}\frac{y}{r}\frac{dp}{dr}.$$

Multiplying the first by y, the second by x and subtracting,

250) $$\frac{d^2\omega}{dr^2} + \frac{3}{r}\frac{d\omega}{dr} = 0,$$

a differential equation whose solution is

251) $$\omega = \frac{a}{r^2} + b.$$

Determining the constants so that $\omega = 0$ for $r = R_1$ and $\omega = \Omega$ for $r = R_2$,

252) $$\omega = \frac{\Omega R_2^{\,2}}{R_1^{\,2} - R_2^{\,2}}\left\{\frac{R_1^{\,2}}{r^2} - 1\right\}.$$

Multiplying equations 249) by x and y respectively, and adding, we have to determine p,

253) $$\varrho\omega^2 r = \frac{dp}{dr}.$$

For the stresses we obtain, using equations 230),

$$X_n = \left(-p - 2\mu\frac{xy}{r}\frac{d\omega}{dr}\right)\cos(nx) + \mu\left(\frac{x^2 - y^2}{r}\frac{d\omega}{dr}\right)\cos(ny),$$

$$254)\quad Y_n = \mu\left(\frac{x^2 - y^2}{r}\frac{d\omega}{dr}\right)\cos(nx) + \left(-p + 2\mu\frac{xy}{r}\frac{d\omega}{dr}\right)\cos(ny),$$

$$Z_n = -p\cos(nz) = 0.$$

This shows that there is a normal pressure p, together with a tangential stress which we obtain by resolving along the tangent,

$$255)\quad T = Y_n\cos(nx) - X_n\cos(ny)$$

$$= \mu\frac{d\omega}{dr}\left\{\frac{x^2 - y^2}{r}(\cos^2 nx - \cos^2 ny) + \frac{4xy}{r}\cos(nx)\cos(ny)\right\}$$

and since $\cos(nx) = \frac{x}{r}$, $\cos(ny) = \frac{y}{r}$,

$$256)\quad T = \mu r\frac{d\omega}{dr} = -\frac{2\mu\Omega R_1^{\,2}R_2^{\,2}}{(R_1^{\,2} - R_2^{\,2})}\frac{1}{r^2}.$$

The moment of the tangential stress on the cylinder of radius r and unit length, is accordingly

$$257)\quad 2\pi r T\cdot r = -\frac{4\pi\mu\Omega R_1^{\,2}R_2^{\,2}}{R_1^{\,2} - R_2^{\,2}}.$$

We may accordingly use this method to determine the viscosity, as is in fact done in apparatus for the testing of lubricants. We see that if the linear dimensions are multiplied in a certain ratio, the moment is increased in the square of that ratio. We also see that the moment of the force required to twist the cylinder is independent of the pressure p, which contains an arbitrary constant, not given by the equation 253), but depending on the hydrostatic pressure applied at the ends.

Let us now consider some simple cases where the flow is not steady, limiting ourselves to the case of small velocities, so that the terms in 233) involving the first space derivatives, being of the second order, are negligible. Let us once more consider laminar flow, defined by equations 234), 235). Let us also put $p = const.$ Instead of 236) we now have for the first of equations 233),

$$258)\quad \frac{\partial u}{\partial t} = \nu\frac{\partial^2 u}{\partial y^2}.$$

This equation is the same as that which represents the conduction of heat in one direction. Let us first consider a solution periodic in the time, such as may be realized physically by the harmonic small oscillation in its own plane of a material lamina constituting the plane $y = 0$, along which the liquid does not slip. We may take as a particular solution

$$e^{my+nt},$$

which inserted in 258) gives

$$n = \nu m^2.$$

If this is to be periodic in t, n must be pure imaginary, say $n = ip$.

Then we have

$$m = \sqrt{\frac{ip}{\nu}} = \pm (1+i)\sqrt{\frac{p}{2\nu}},$$

and

$$e^{\pm\sqrt{\frac{p}{2\nu}}y + i\left(pt \pm \sqrt{\frac{p}{2\nu}}y\right)},$$

of which complex quantity both the real and the imaginary parts must separately satisfy the equation 258), when multiplied by arbitrary constants. Let us accordingly take

$$259)\quad u = \left\{A\cos\left(pt - \sqrt{\frac{p}{2\nu}}\cdot y\right) + B\sin\left(pt - \sqrt{\frac{p}{2\nu}}y\right)\right\}e^{-\sqrt{\frac{p}{2\nu}}\cdot y}.$$

This represents a wave of frequency $\frac{p}{2\pi}$ and wave-length $2\pi\sqrt{\frac{2\nu}{p}}$ travelling with velocity $\sqrt{2\nu p}$, which as we see varies as the square root of the frequency. Unlike our waves in perfect fluids however it falls off in amplitude, being rapidly damped as we go into the fluid, being reduced in the ratio $e^{-2\pi} = \frac{1}{535}$ in each wave-length. Thus such motions are propagated but a short distance into a fluid. In a similar manner the absorption of light by non-transparent media is explained, the ether there having the properties of a viscous *solid*.

If we treat the equations 233) in the same way as we did 27) in obtaining equation 57), § 191, we obtain instead the following,

$$260)\quad \begin{aligned} \frac{d}{dt}\left(\frac{\xi}{\varrho}\right) &= \frac{\xi}{\varrho}\frac{\partial u}{\partial x} + \frac{\eta}{\varrho}\frac{\partial u}{\partial y} + \frac{\zeta}{\varrho}\frac{\partial u}{\partial z} + \nu\Delta\xi,\\ \frac{d}{dt}\left(\frac{\eta}{\varrho}\right) &= \frac{\xi}{\varrho}\frac{\partial v}{\partial x} + \frac{\eta}{\varrho}\frac{\partial v}{\partial y} + \frac{\zeta}{\varrho}\frac{\partial v}{\partial z} + \nu\Delta\eta,\\ \frac{d}{dt}\left(\frac{\zeta}{\varrho}\right) &= \frac{\xi}{\varrho}\frac{\partial w}{\partial x} + \frac{\eta}{\varrho}\frac{\partial w}{\partial y} + \frac{\zeta}{\varrho}\frac{\partial w}{\partial z} + \nu\Delta\zeta. \end{aligned}$$

Under the circumstances of slow motions these also reduce to

$$261)\quad \begin{aligned} \frac{\partial\xi}{\partial t} &= \mu\Delta\xi,\\ \frac{\partial\eta}{\partial t} &= \mu\Delta\eta,\\ \frac{\partial\zeta}{\partial t} &= \mu\Delta\zeta. \end{aligned}$$

Thus we see that the three components of the vorticity are propagated independently, each according to the equation for the conduction of

heat. The example just treated is an example of this, for we find at once

262) $$\xi = \eta = 0, \quad \zeta = -\frac{1}{2}\frac{\partial u}{\partial y},$$

and the vorticity is propagated like the velocity.

As a final example, let us consider a case of laminar motion in which u, as a function of y, has a discontinuity, this having an important application to the theory of thin plane jets and flames, including sensitive flames.[1]) We will suppose that at the time $t = 0$ for $y < 0$ u has a certain constant value, and that for $y > 0$ it has a different constant value. It is easy to see that this is equivalent to supposing that there is no vorticity except in an infinitely thin lamina at $y = 0$. For we have

263) $$\int_{-\varepsilon}^{\varepsilon} \zeta\, dy = -\frac{1}{2}\int_{-\varepsilon}^{\varepsilon} \frac{\partial u}{\partial y}\, dy = \frac{1}{2}(u_1 - u_2)$$

where u_1 is the velocity on one side, u_2 that on the other of the layer of thickness 2ε. Now if the thickness decrease without limit, while ζ increases without limit, the integral may still be finite, as we shall suppose.

We have then to find two solutions u and ζ of equation 258), so related that $\zeta = -\frac{1}{2}\frac{\partial u}{\partial y}$. Let us put $s = \frac{y}{\sqrt{t}}$, and try to find a particular solution that is a function of s alone. We have

264) $$\begin{aligned} \frac{\partial u}{\partial t} &= \frac{du}{ds}\frac{\partial s}{\partial t} = -\frac{1}{2}\frac{du}{ds}\frac{y}{\sqrt{t^3}}, \\ \frac{\partial u}{\partial y} &= \frac{du}{ds}\frac{\partial s}{\partial y} = \frac{du}{ds}\frac{1}{\sqrt{t}}, \\ \frac{\partial^2 u}{\partial y^2} &= \frac{1}{\sqrt{t}}\frac{d^2 u}{ds^2}\frac{\partial s}{\partial y} = \frac{1}{t}\frac{d^2 u}{ds^2}, \end{aligned}$$

so that our equation becomes the ordinary differential equation,

265) $$-\frac{1}{2} s \frac{du}{ds} = \mu \frac{d^2 u}{ds^2},$$

or

266) $$\frac{d}{ds}\left(\log \frac{du}{ds}\right) = -\frac{s}{2\mu}.$$

---

1) Rayleigh, *On the Stability, or Instability, of certain Fluid Motions* Proc. London Math. Soc., xi., pp. 57—70, 1880. Scientific Papers, Vol. I, p. 474.

The integral of this equation is given by

$$267)\quad \log\frac{du}{ds} = -\frac{s^2}{4\mu} + const.,\quad \frac{du}{ds} = ce^{-\frac{s^2}{4\mu}},\quad u = c\int e^{-\frac{s^2}{4\mu}}ds.$$

The last indicated quadrature cannot be effected except by development of the integrand in series, but if we take for the lower limit the value zero, we may express u in terms of the so-called error-function, occurring in the theory of probability,

$$268)\qquad Erf(x) = \int_0^x e^{-x^2}dx.$$

Tables of the values of $Erf(x)$ have been calculated, and are found in treatises on probability. (Lord Kelvin reprints one such on p. 434 of Vol. 3 of his collected papers.) Since the integrand is an even function of x, it is evident that $Erf(x)$ is an odd function of its upper limit x. It may be easily shown that the definite integral between zero and infinity has the value $\frac{\sqrt{\pi}}{2}$, so that putting $x^2 = \frac{s^2}{4\mu}$, and adding a constant, we have

$$269)\qquad u = \frac{u_2 + u_1}{2} + \frac{u_2 - u_1}{\sqrt{\pi}}\int_0^{\frac{y}{2\sqrt{\mu t}}} e^{-x^2}dx.$$

This determination of the constants makes, for *all* positive values of y and for $t = 0$, $u = u_1$ (the upper limit being $+\infty$), and for *all* negative values $u = u_2$, thus giving the discontinuity required at $y = 0$. For all other values of t however, no matter how small, the values from the negative side run smoothly into those on the positive, showing how the discontinuity is instantly lost. This is shown in Fig. 171, in which successive curves show values of u at times equal to 1, 2, 3, 4, 5, 6 times $\frac{1}{\mu}$.

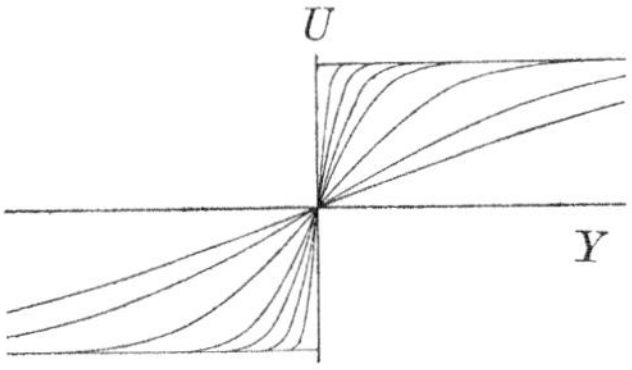

Fig. 171.

Differentiating by the limit, we find

$$270)\qquad \zeta = -\frac{1}{2}\frac{\partial u}{\partial y} = \frac{u_1 - u_2}{4\sqrt{\pi\mu t}}e^{-\frac{y^2}{4\mu t}},$$

which is infinite when $t=0$, $\frac{y}{\sqrt{t}}=0$, as we supposed, but which immediately drops to a finite value, and, no matter what the value of y, immediately acquires values different from zero. Thus the

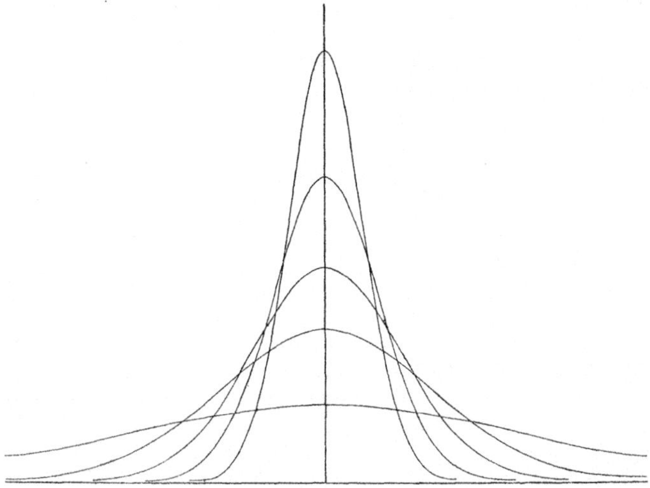

Fig. 172.

vorticity, originally confined within the infinitely thin sheet of discontinuity, is instantaneously distributed throughout the liquid, as shown in Fig. 172, for the times $\frac{1}{8}, \frac{1}{4}, \frac{1}{2}$, 1, 4 times $\frac{1}{\mu}$. Thus we see how discontinuities of the sort shown in Fig. 166 are impossible in nature, being replaced by the formation of eddies.

NOTES.

NOTE I.

DIFFERENTIAL EQUATIONS.

The differential equations of mechanics are of the type known as *ordinary*, as opposed to *partial*, that is they involve a number of functions of a single variable, the time, and the derivatives of these functions with respect to that variable. Suppose for simplicity that we have three functions x, y, z of the variable t, and that instead of being given explicitly, they are defined by the equations

$$1) \quad F_1(x, y, z, t) = 0, \quad F_2(x, y, z, t) = 0, \quad F_3(x, y, z, t) = 0.$$

If we now differentiate these equations, bearing in mind that x, y, z are dependent on t, we obtain

$$2) \quad \begin{aligned} \frac{\partial F_1}{\partial x}\frac{dx}{dt} + \frac{\partial F_1}{\partial y}\frac{dy}{dt} + \frac{\partial F_1}{\partial z}\frac{dz}{dt} + \frac{\partial F_1}{\partial t} &= 0, \\ \frac{\partial F_2}{\partial x}\frac{dx}{dt} + \frac{\partial F_2}{\partial y}\frac{dy}{dt} + \frac{\partial F_2}{\partial z}\frac{dz}{dt} + \frac{\partial F_2}{\partial t} &= 0, \\ \frac{\partial F_3}{\partial x}\frac{dx}{dt} + \frac{\partial F_3}{\partial y}\frac{dy}{dt} + \frac{\partial F_3}{\partial z}\frac{dz}{dt} + \frac{\partial F_3}{\partial t} &= 0. \end{aligned}$$

Suppose now that the functions F contained, besides the variables indicated, certain constants, $c_1, c_2 \ldots$ Each time that we obtain an equation by differentiation, we may utilize it in order to eliminate from the equations 1) one of the constants c. Thus we obtain (since the *partial* derivatives are given functions of x, y, z, t), instead of the equations 1), the following,

$$3) \quad G_1\left(x, y, z, t, \frac{dx}{dt}, \frac{dy}{dt}, \frac{dz}{dt}\right) = 0, \quad G_2\left(x, \ldots \frac{dz}{dt}\right) = 0, \quad G_3\left(x, \ldots \frac{dz}{dt}\right) = 0,$$

which, since they contain the derivatives $\frac{dx}{dt}, \frac{dy}{dt}, \frac{dz}{dt}$, are *differential* equations, of which equations 1) are said to be *integrals*.

If we again differentiate equations 2), we obtain

$$4) \quad \frac{\partial F_1}{\partial x}\frac{d^2 x}{dt^2} + \frac{\partial^2 F_1}{\partial x^2}\left(\frac{dx}{dt}\right)^2 + 2\frac{\partial^2 F_1}{\partial x \partial y}\frac{dx}{dt}\frac{dy}{dt} + \cdots = 0, \text{ etc.,}$$

which we may again use to eliminate constants c from 3), so that instead of 1) or 3) we now have the system

$$5)\qquad \begin{aligned} &H_1\left(x, y, z, t, \frac{dx}{dt}, \frac{dy}{dt}, \frac{dz}{dt}, \frac{d^2x}{dt^2}, \frac{d^2y}{dt^2}, \frac{d^2z}{dt^2}\right) = 0, \\ &H_2\left(x, y, z, t, \ldots\ldots\ldots\ldots\ldots \frac{d^2z}{dt}\right) = 0, \\ &H_3\left(x, y, z, t, \ldots\ldots\ldots\ldots\ldots \frac{d^2z}{ct^2}\right) = 0. \end{aligned}$$

These differential equations, since the order of the derivatives of the highest order contained in them is the second, are said to be of the second order. In like manner we may continue, and successively eliminate all the constants $c_1, c_2 \ldots$, obtaining differential equations of successively higher orders. Reversing the process, each set of a given order is said to be the *integral* of the set of order next higher.

Any of the sets of differential equations represents the functions x, y, z, but with the following distinction. If the equations 1) contain constants, to which different values may be assigned,

$$6)\quad F_1(x, y, z, t, c_1, c_2 \ldots c_n) = 0, \quad F_2(x, y, z, t, c_1, c_2 \ldots c_n) = 0,$$
$$F_3(x, y, z, t, c_1, c_2 \ldots c_n) = 0,$$

for every set of values that may be assigned to the constants, a different set of functions is represented, so that we have an infinity of different functions, the order of the infinity being the number of constants contained in the equations. Now the differential equations obtained by eliminating the arbitrary constants represent all the functions obtained by giving the constants any set of values whatever. Thus the information contained in the differential equations is in a sense more general than that contained in the equations 6), in which we give the constants any particular values.

If we reverse the process which we have here followed to form the differential equations, we see that every time that we succeed, by integration, in making derivatives of a certain order disappear, we introduce at the same time a number of arbitrary constants equal to the number of derivatives which disappear. Thus the integral equations of a set of differential equations of any order will contain a number of arbitrary constants equal to the order of the differential equations multiplied by the number of dependent variables. As an example consider the very simple case of equations 38), § 13.

$$38)\qquad \frac{d^2x}{dt^2} = 0, \quad \frac{d^2y}{dt^2} = 0, \quad \frac{d^2z}{dt^2} = 0.$$

Integrating these we obtain

$$39)\qquad x = c_1t + d_1, \quad y = c_2t + d_2, \quad z = c_3t + d_3,$$

containing the six arbitrary constants $c_1, c_2, c_3, d_1, d_2, d_3$. The meaning of these integral equations is that the point x, y, z describes a straight line with a constant velocity. But the differential equations 38) represent

the motion of a point describing any line in space with any velocity. Now there are a four-fold infinity of lines in space, and a single infinity of velocities. We therefore see the very general nature of the information contained in the differential equations. So in the example of § 13 the statement that all the planets experience an acceleration toward the sun which is proportional to the inverse square of the distance expresses a very general and simple truth, in the form of a set of differential equations, while the integral states that the planets describe some conic section in some plane through the sun, in some periodic time, all the particulars of which statement are arbitrary.

The characteristic property of the differential equations of mechanics, for the phenomena furnished us by Nature, is apparently that they are of the second order. This, although leaving possibilities of great generality, suffices to limit natural phenomena to a certain class, in contrast to what would be conceivable. For the consequences of the removal of this limitation, the student is referred to the very interesting work by Königsberger, *Die Principien der Mechanik.*

In order to determine the particular values of the arbitrary constants applicable to any particular problem, some data must be given in addition to the differential equations. It is customary to furnish these by stating for a particular instant of time, the values of the coordinates of each point of the system, and of their first time-derivatives, which amounts to specifying for each point its position and its vector velocity for the particular instant in question. This furnishes six data for each independent point, which is just sufficient to determine the constants. Thus if we are dealing with a system of n points free to move in any manner, under the action of any forces, the statement of the problem will consist in the giving of the differential equations

$$F_1\left(x_1,\ y_1,\ z_1,\ x_2,\ y_2\ \ldots\ z_n,\ t,\ \frac{dx}{dt},\ \ldots\ \frac{dz_n}{dt},\ \frac{d^2x}{dt^2},\ \ldots\ \frac{d^2z_n}{dt^2}\right),$$

$$F_2\left(x_1,\ \ldots\ldots\ldots\ldots\ldots\ldots\ldots\ \frac{d^2z_n}{dt^2}\right),$$

$$\ldots\ldots\ldots\ldots\ldots\ldots\ldots\ldots\ldots\ldots$$

$$\ldots\ldots\ldots\ldots\ldots\ldots\ldots\ldots\ldots\ldots$$

$$F_{3n}\left(x_1,\ \ldots\ldots\ldots\ldots\ldots\ldots\ldots\ \frac{d^2z_n}{dt^2}\right),$$

together with the so-called initial conditions, that for $t = t_0$,

$$x_1 = x_1^{\ 0},\quad y_1 = y_1^{\ 0}\ \ldots\ \ldots\ z_n = z_n^{\ 0}$$

$$\frac{dx_1}{dt} = [x'_1]^0,\ \frac{dy_1}{dt} = [y'_1]^0,\ \cdots\ \frac{dz_n}{dt} = [z'_n]^0.$$

From these it is required to find the integrals

$$x_1 = f_1(t),\ y_1 = f_2(t),\ z_1 = f_3(t),\ \ldots\ z_n = f_{3n}(t).$$

Cases involving the motion of points whose freedom of motion is limited are dealt with in subsequent chapters.

NOTE II.

ALGEBRA OF INDETERMINATE MULTIPLIERS.

On page 61 we have an example of the use of indeterminate multipliers in elimination. It may be somewhat more clear if we examine in just what the process involved consists. Equation (12) is a linear equation involving the $3n$ quantities $\delta x_1, \ldots \delta z_n$, each multiplied by a coefficient which is independent of the δ's. Besides this equation the quantities δ satisfy the equations 14), which are of the same form, that is, linear in all the δ's, with coefficients independent of them. Aside from this the δ's may have any values whatever. It is for the purposes of this discussion quite immaterial that the δ's are small quantities, we are concerned simply with a question of elimination. Let us accordingly represent them by the letters $x_1, x_2, \ldots x_m$, between which we have the linear equation

$$1)\qquad A_1x_1 + A_2x_2 + \cdots + A_mx_m = 0.$$

The x's are however not independent, but must in addition satisfy the equations

$$2)\qquad \begin{aligned} B_{11}x_1 + B_{12}x_2 \cdots + B_{1m}x_m &= 0, \\ B_{21}x_1 + B_{22}x_2 \cdots + B_{2m}x_m &= 0, \\ \cdots\cdots\cdots\cdots\cdots & \\ B_{k1}x_1 + B_{k2}x_2 \cdots + B_{km}x_m &= 0. \end{aligned}$$

The number of these equations, k, is less than m, the number of the x's. The question is now, what relations are involved among the A's and B's when the x's have any values whatever compatible with the equations 2).

We may evidently proceed as follows. Transposing $m-k$ terms in 2), say the last, we may solve the equations for the quantities $x_1, x_2 \ldots x_k$, as linear functions of the remaining $x_{k+1}, \ldots x_m$. These $m-k$ quantities are now perfectly arbitrary. Inserting the values of $x_1 \ldots x_k$ in equation 1), this becomes linear in the $m-k$ quantities $x_{k+1}, \ldots x_m$, which being purely arbitrary, in order for equation 1) to hold for all values of the x's, the coefficient of each must vanish, giving us the required $m-k$ relations between the A's and B's.

Instead of proceeding in the manner described, the method of Lagrange is to multiply the equations 2) respectively by multipliers $\lambda_1, \lambda_2, \ldots \lambda_k$, to which any convenient value may be given, and then to add them to equation 1). We thus obtain

$$3)\qquad \begin{aligned} &(A_1 + \lambda_1 B_{11} + \lambda_2 B_{21} \cdots + \lambda_k B_{k1})x_1 \\ +\, &(A_2 + \lambda_1 B_{12} + \lambda_2 B_{22} \cdots + \lambda_k B_{k2})x_2 \\ &\cdots\cdots\cdots\cdots\cdots\cdots \\ +\, &(A_m + \lambda_1 B_{1m} + \lambda_2 B_{2m} \cdots + \lambda_k B_{km})x_m = 0. \end{aligned}$$

In this equation the x's are not all arbitrary, but as before k may be determined as linear functions of the remainder, say $x_1, \ldots x_k$ in terms of $x_{k+1}, \ldots x_m$, which are arbitrary. But the multipliers λ are as yet arbitrary. Let us determine them so that they satisfy the equations

$$4)\qquad \begin{aligned} &A_1 + \lambda_1 B_{11} + \lambda_2 B_{21} \cdots + \lambda_k B_{k1} = 0, \\ &A_2 + \lambda_1 B_{12} + \lambda_2 B_{22} \cdots + \lambda_k B_{k2} = 0, \\ &\cdots\cdots\cdots\cdots\cdots \\ &A_k + \lambda_1 B_{1k} + \lambda_2 B_{2k} \cdots + \lambda_k B_{kk} = 0, \end{aligned}$$

which are just sufficient to determine them. We thus have

$$5)\qquad \begin{aligned} &(A_{k+1} + \lambda_1 B_{1,k+1} + \cdots + \lambda_k B_{k,k+1}) x_{k+1} \\ &\cdots\cdots\cdots\cdots\cdots \\ &+ (A_m + \lambda_1 B_{1m} + \cdots + \lambda_k B_{km}) x_m = 0, \end{aligned}$$

in which the x's are all arbitrary, so that the $m - k$ coefficients must vanish, giving the $m - k$ equations.

$$6)\qquad \begin{aligned} &A_{k+1} + \lambda_1 B_{1,k+1} + \cdots + \lambda_k B_{k,k+1} = 0 \\ &\cdots\cdots\cdots\cdots\cdots \\ &A_m + \lambda_1 B_{1m} + \cdots + \lambda_k B_{km} = 0. \end{aligned}$$

Inserting in these the values of the λ's already found, we have the $m - k$ required relations between the A's and B's. Obviously the result of the elimination may be expressed in the form obtained by writing equal to zero each of the determinants of order $k + 1$ obtained from the array of A's and B's in equations 4) and 5) by omitting $m - k - 1$ rows, only $m - k$ of the determinants thus obtained being independent.

NOTE III.

QUADRATIC DIFFERENTIAL FORMS. GENERALIZED VECTORS.

The method of transforming the equations of motion used in § 37 and the application of hyperspace there occurring render a somewhat more detailed treatment of the question desirable. In order to elucidate matters, we will begin with the very simple case of a space which is included in ordinary space, namely the space of two dimensions forming the surface characterized by two coordinates q_1, q_2, as on page 110. We have seen that this space is completely characterized by the expression for the arc as the quadratic differential form

$$1)\qquad ds^2 = E\,dq_1^2 + 2F\,dq_1\,dq_2 + G\,dq_2^2.$$

A point lying on this surface may be displaced in any manner, in or out of the surface. If it is displaced in the surface, its displacement is a vector belonging to the two-dimensional space considered. We will

call the changes dq_1, dq_2 the *coordinates* of the displacement. We have found that when the displacement is made so as to change only one of the coordinates of the point q_1 or q_2, the arcs are respectively $ds_1 = \sqrt{E}\, dq_1$, $ds_2 = \sqrt{G}\, dq_2$, and that the angle included by them is given by

$$\cos \vartheta = \frac{F}{\sqrt{EG}}.$$

If now we have any displacement ds, whose coordinates are dq_1, dq_2, and project it orthogonally upon the directions of ds_1, ds_2, we easily see (Fig. 26) that the projections $d\sigma_1, d\sigma_2$ are

$$2)\quad \begin{aligned} d\sigma_1 &= ds_1 + ds_2 \cos\vartheta = \sqrt{E}\, dq_1 + \frac{F\sqrt{G}\, dq_2}{\sqrt{EG}} = \frac{E\, dq_1 + F\, dq_2}{\sqrt{E}}, \\ d\sigma_2 &= ds_2 + ds_1 \cos\vartheta = \sqrt{G}\, dq_2 + \frac{F\sqrt{E}\, dq_1}{\sqrt{EG}} = \frac{F\, dq_1 + G\, dq_1}{\sqrt{G}}. \end{aligned}$$

We shall now, following Hertz, introduce the *reduced component* of the displacement along either coordinate-line, defined as the orthogoneal projection divided by the rate of change of the coordinate with respect to the distance traveled in its own direction. These reduced components we shall denote by a bar, so that

$$3)\quad \begin{aligned} d\bar{q}_1 &= \frac{d\sigma_1}{\frac{dq_1}{ds_1}} = E\, dq_1 + F\, dq_2, \\ d\bar{q}_2 &= \frac{d\sigma_2}{\frac{dq_2}{ds_2}} = F\, dq_1 + G\, dq_2. \end{aligned}$$

The fundamental property of these reduced components is found in the equation giving the magnitude of the displacement

$$4)\quad ds^2 = dq_1\, d\bar{q}_1 + dq_2\, d\bar{q}_2,$$

that is the square of an infinitesimal displacement is the sum of products of each coordinate of the displacement multiplied by the respective reduced component.

In like manner the geometric product of two different displacements ds, ds', whose coordinates are dq_1, dq_2, dq_1', dq_2' is found to be

$$5)\quad \begin{aligned} ds\, ds' \cos(ds, ds') &= dx\, dx' + dy\, dy' + dz\, dz' \\ &= \left(\frac{\partial x}{\partial q_1} dq_1 + \frac{\partial x}{\partial q_2} dq_2\right)\left(\frac{\partial x}{\partial q_1} dq_1' + \frac{\partial x}{\partial q_2} dq_2'\right) \\ &+ \left(\frac{\partial y}{\partial q_1} dq_1 + \frac{\partial y}{\partial q_2} dq_2\right)\left(\frac{\partial y}{\partial q_1} dq_1' + \frac{\partial y}{\partial q_2} dq_2'\right) \\ &+ \left(\frac{\partial z}{\partial q_1} dq_1 + \frac{\partial z}{\partial q_2} dq_2\right)\left(\frac{\partial z}{\partial q_1} dq_1' + \frac{\partial z}{\partial q_2} dq_2'\right) \\ &= E\, dq_1\, dq_1' + F(dq_1\, dq_2' + dq_2\, dq_1') + G\, dq_2\, dq_2' \\ &= dq_1\, d\bar{q}_1' + dq_2\, d\bar{q}_2' = dq_1'\, d\bar{q}_1 + dq_2'\, d\bar{q}_2. \end{aligned}$$

The geometric product of two displacements is equal to the sum of products of the coordinates of either vector by the reduced components of the other. Thus the geometric product is defined by means of the quadratic differential form 1) defining the space in question.

Solving the equations 3) for dq_1, dq_2, we obtain

$$6)\quad \begin{aligned} dq_1 &= \frac{G\,d\bar{q}_1 - F\,d\bar{q}_2}{EG - F^2} = R_{11}\,d\bar{q}_1 + R_{12}\,d\bar{q}_2 \\ dq_2 &= -\frac{F\,d\bar{q}_1 - E\,d\bar{q}_2}{EG - F_2} = R_{12}\,d\bar{q}_1 + R_{22}\,d\bar{q}_2, \end{aligned}$$

from which we obtain

$$7)\quad ds^2 = R_{11}\,d\bar{q}_1^{\,2} + 2\,R_{12}\,d\bar{q}_1\,d\bar{q}_2 + R_{22}\,d\bar{q}_2^{\,2}.$$

The expression 7) is called the reciprocal form to 1). Corresponding to it we obtain the form of the geometric product

$$8)\quad ds\,ds'\cos(ds_, ds') = R_{11}\,d\bar{q}_1\,d\bar{q}_1' + R_{12}(d\bar{q}_1\,d\bar{q}_2' + d\bar{q}_2\,d\bar{q}_1') + R_{22}\,d\bar{q}_2\,d\bar{q}_2'.$$

We may now define any vector belonging to the space considered, as one whose components have the same properties as those possessed by those of an infinitesimal displacement. Suppose that X, Y, Z are the rectangular components of a vector R, it does not belong to the space 1) unless it is tangent to the surface in question. If so, we have a displacement such that

$$9)\quad \frac{R}{ds} = \frac{X}{dx} = \frac{Y}{dy} = \frac{Z}{dz} = \frac{Q_1}{dq_1} = \frac{Q_2}{dq_2} = \frac{1}{\varepsilon}.$$

Then Q_1, Q_2 are the coordinates of the vector in the system q_1, q_2, and the magnitude of the vector is given by the equations

$$10)\quad \begin{aligned} R^2 = X^2 + Y^2 + Z^2 &= \frac{1}{\varepsilon^2}(dx^2 + dy^2 + dz^2) \\ &= \frac{1}{\varepsilon^2}(E\,dq_1^{\,2} + 2F\,dq_1\,dq_2 + G\,dq_2^{\,2}) \\ &= EQ_1^{\,2} + 2FQ_1Q_2 + GQ_2^{\,2} \\ &= Q_1\bar{Q}_1 + Q_2\bar{Q}_2, \end{aligned}$$

where

$$11)\quad \begin{aligned} \bar{Q}_1 &= EQ_1 + FQ_2 \\ \bar{Q}_2 &= FQ_1 + GQ_2 \end{aligned}$$

are its reduced components belonging to its coordinates Q_1, Q_2. The geometric product of two vectors R, R' is

$$12)\quad Q_1\bar{Q}_1' + Q_2\bar{Q}_2' = Q_1'\bar{Q}_1 + Q_2'\bar{Q}_2.$$

If now one of the vectors is finite, the other an infinitesimal displacement, we have the geometric product

$$13)\quad \begin{aligned} R\,ds\cos(R, ds) &= X\,dx + Y\,dy + Z\,dz = \bar{Q}_1\,dq_1 + \bar{Q}_2\,dq_2 \\ &= \left(X\frac{\partial x}{\partial q_1} + Y\frac{\partial y}{\partial q_1} + Z\frac{\partial z}{\partial q_1}\right)dq_1 + \left(X\frac{\partial x}{\partial q_2} + Y\frac{\partial y}{\partial q_2} + Z\frac{\partial z}{\partial q_2}\right)dq_2. \end{aligned}$$

Thus the reduced components $\overline{Q}_1, \overline{Q}_2$ are given by the definition which we have adopted on page 116, equation 42).

Having now illustrated the subject by a space of two dimensions, we can easily extend our notions to space of any number of dimensions m, defined by the form

14) $$ds^2 = \sum_{r=1}^{r=m} \sum_{s=1}^{s=m} Q_{rs}\, dq_r\, dq_s.$$

For any one of the coordinate directions we have

15) $$ds_r^2 = Q_{rr}\, dq_r^2,$$

and for the geometric product of two displacements,

16) $$ds\, ds' \cos(ds,\ ds') = \sum^r \sum^s Q_{rs}\, dq_r\, dq_s'.$$

If one is in the direction ds_r, all dq's being 0 except dq_r,

17) $$ds\, ds_r \cos(ds,\ ds_r) = \sum^s Q_{rs}\, dq_r\, dq_s,$$

and dividing by ds_r we obtain the orthogonal projection of ds on ds_r

18) $$d\sigma_r = ds \cos(ds,\ ds_r) = \frac{\Sigma^s Q_{rs}\, dq_s}{\sqrt{Q_{rr}}\, dq_r},$$

from which we obtain by the definition of the reduced component

19) $$d\overline{q}_r = \frac{d\sigma_r}{\frac{dq_r}{ds_r}} = \sum^s Q_{rs}\, dq_s.$$

We have as before

20) $$ds^2 = \sum^r dq_r\, d\overline{q}_r,$$

21) $$ds\, ds' \cos(ds,\ ds') = \sum^r \sum^s dq_r\, d\overline{q}_s,$$

and if the solution of 19) is

22) $$dq_r = \sum^s R_{rs}\, d\overline{q}_s,$$

we have the reciprocal form

23) $$ds^2 = \sum^r \sum^s R_{rs}\, d\overline{q}_r\, d\overline{q}_s.$$

Again we may define a vector belonging to the hyperspace considered, and now the rectangular components may be of any number, the limitation of the vector to the space in question reducing the number of generalized

components to accord with the number of dimensions of the hyperspace. The geometric product of the vector with an infinitesimal displacement defines the generalized coordinates of the vector, so that

$$\sum_{r=1}^{r=n} (X_r dx_r + Y_r dy_r + Z_r dz_r)$$

$$= \sum_{r=1}^{r=n} \sum_{s=1}^{s=m} \left(X_r \frac{\partial x_r}{\partial q_s} + Y_r \frac{\partial y_r}{\partial q_s} + Z_r \frac{\partial z_r}{\partial q_s} \right) dq_s = \sum_{s=1}^{s=m} P_s dq_s,$$

and we find that the *reduced component* of the vector is what is defined by the formula 42) of page 116)

In our application to mechanics the differential form in question is $2Tdt^2$, where T is the kinetic energy of the system It is immaterial whether we speak of vectors in a hyperspace, as we have here done, or, as Hertz does, speak of vectors with respect to our mechanical system. The meaning in either case is plain. On dividing the above formulae by dt^2, we find that the generalized velocities and momenta have the relation to each other of coordinates and reduced components of the same vector in the hyperspace. The two reciprocal forms 14) and 23) have the relation of the Lagrangian and Hamiltonian forms of the kinetic energy. The equations of motion of the system say that, no matter how the forces are applied, or how parts of them are equilibrated by the constraints, the *reduced components* of the applied and the effective forces are equal for every coordinate.

NOTE IV.

AXES OF CENTRAL QUADRIC.

The principal axes of a central quadric surface,

1) $F(x, y, z) \equiv Ax^2 + By^2 + Cz^2 + 2Dyz + 2Ezx + 2Fxy = 1,$

are defined as the radii vectores in the directions for which the radius vector is a maximum or minimum. If we put

$$x = r\alpha, \qquad y = r\beta, \qquad z = r\gamma,$$

we have

2) $$\frac{1}{r^2} = F(\alpha, \beta, \gamma),$$

and the maxima and minima of r occurring for the same directions as the minima and maxima of $1/r^2$, are obtained by finding the maxima and minima of $F(\alpha, \beta, \gamma)$ subject to the condition

3) $$\varphi(\alpha, \beta, \gamma) \equiv \alpha^2 + \beta^2 + \gamma^2 - 1 = 0.$$

If we multiply this equation by an arbitrary constant $-\lambda$ and add it to $F(\alpha, \beta, \gamma)$, we obtain the condition by writing the derivatives of $F-\lambda\varphi$ equal to zero Thus we obtain

$$4)\qquad \begin{aligned} \frac{\partial F}{\partial \alpha} - 2\lambda\alpha &= 0, \\ \frac{\partial F}{\partial \beta} - 2\lambda\beta &= 0, \\ \frac{\partial F}{\partial \gamma} - 2\lambda\gamma &= 0. \end{aligned}$$

Now the direction cosines of the normal to the quadric at a point x, y, z are proportional to

$$\frac{\partial F}{\partial x}, \quad \frac{\partial F}{\partial y}, \quad \frac{\partial F}{\partial z}.$$

At points where the normal is in the direction of the radius vector we have

$$\frac{\frac{\partial F}{\partial x}}{x} = \frac{\frac{\partial F}{\partial y}}{y} = \frac{\frac{\partial F}{\partial z}}{z}.$$

But

$$\frac{\frac{\partial F(x, y, z)}{\partial x}}{x} = \frac{\frac{\partial F(\alpha, \beta, \gamma)}{\partial \alpha}}{\alpha} \quad \text{etc.,}$$

so that the equations 4) show that at the ends of the principal axes the tangent plane is perpendicular to the radius vector.

Effecting the differentiations the equations 4) become

$$5)\qquad \begin{aligned} (A-\lambda)\alpha + F\beta \quad + E\gamma \quad &= 0, \\ F\alpha + (B-\lambda)\beta + D\gamma \quad &= 0, \\ E\alpha + D\beta \quad + (C-\lambda)\gamma &= 0. \end{aligned}$$

The condition that these equations, linear in α, β, γ, shall be compatible for values of α, β, γ, other than zero is that the determinant of the coefficients shall vanish.

$$6)\qquad \begin{vmatrix} A-\lambda, & F\,, & E \\ F\,, & B-\lambda, & D \\ E\,, & D\,, & C-\lambda \end{vmatrix} = 0.$$

This is a cubic in λ, which being expanded is

$$7)\qquad \begin{aligned} f(\lambda) \equiv (A-\lambda)(B-\lambda)(C-\lambda) - D^2(A-\lambda) - E^2(B-\lambda) \\ - F^2(C-\lambda) + 2DEF = 0. \end{aligned}$$

We shall show that this always has three real roots. Put

$$8)\qquad \begin{aligned} A - \lambda &= u + q, \\ B - \lambda &= v + r, \\ C - \lambda &= w + s, \end{aligned}$$

where q, r, s are to be determined later. Then

$$8)\qquad \begin{aligned} &(u + q)(p + r)(w + s) - D^2(u + q) - E^2(v + r) \\ &\qquad - F^2(w + s) + 2DEF = 0 \end{aligned}$$

or arranged according to powers of u, v, w,

$$9)\qquad \begin{aligned} &uvw + qvw + rwu + suv \\ &+ u(rs - D^2) + v(sq - E^2) + w(qr - F^2) \\ &+ qrs + 2DEF - D^2q - E^2r - F^2s = 0. \end{aligned}$$

Let us now determine q, r, s, so as to make the terms of first order in u, v, w vanish.

$$rs = D^2, \quad sq = E^2, \quad qr = F^2,$$

from which by multiplication and division

$$10)\qquad qrs = DEF, \quad q = \frac{EF}{D}, \quad r = \frac{FD}{E}, \quad s = \frac{DE}{F}.$$

Thus there remains

$$11)\qquad uvw + \frac{EF}{D}vw + \frac{FD}{E}wu + \frac{DE}{F}uv = 0.$$

Now from 8)

$$12)\qquad \begin{aligned} u &= A - \lambda - q = A - EF/D - \lambda = a - \lambda, \\ v &= B - \lambda - r = B - FD/E - \lambda = b - \lambda, \\ w &= C - \lambda - s = C - DE/F - \lambda = c - \lambda, \end{aligned}$$

if we write

$$A - EF/D = a, \quad B - FD/E = b, \quad C - DE/F = c.$$

Also since from 10) q, r, s are all of the same sign, let us call them $\pm l^2$, m^2, n^2, so that we have from 11)

$$13)\qquad \begin{aligned} f(\lambda) \equiv (a - \lambda)(b - \lambda)(c - \lambda) &\pm [l^2(b - \lambda)(c - \lambda) \\ &+ m^2(c - \lambda)(a - \lambda) + n^2(a - \lambda)(b - \lambda)]. \end{aligned}$$

Substituting for λ in turn the values $-\infty$, c, b, a, $+\infty$, we obtain

$$14)\qquad \begin{aligned} f(-\infty) &= \infty, \\ f(c) &= \pm n^2(a - c)(b - c) \\ f(b) &= \pm m^2(c - b)(a - b) \\ f(a) &= \pm l^2(b - a)(c - a) \\ f(\infty) &= -\infty. \end{aligned}$$

Let us suppose $a > b > c$, and take the upper sign in 14). Then for

$\lambda = -\infty$	$f(\lambda)$ is $+$
c	$+$
b	$-$
a	$+$
∞	$-$

and the function $f(\lambda)$ behaves as shown in Fig. 13. As there are three changes of sign, there are three real roots. It is to be noticed that the reality of all the roots depends on q, r, s being of the same sign. Let us call the roots λ_1, λ_2, λ_3. Either one of these being inserted in the equations 5), the equations become compatible, and suffice to determine the ratios of the direction cosines. There are therefore always three principal axes to a central quadric surface. If we call the cosines belonging to the roots λ_1, α_1, β_1, γ_1, those belonging to λ_2, α_2, β_2, γ_2, equations 5) become

15)
$$\begin{aligned} \lambda_1\alpha_1 &= A\alpha_1 + F\beta_1 + E\gamma_1, \\ \lambda_1\beta_1 &= F\alpha_1 + B\beta_1 + D\gamma_1, \\ \lambda_1\gamma_1 &= E\alpha_1 + D\beta_1 + C\gamma_1, \\ \lambda_2\alpha_2 &= A\alpha_2 + F\beta_2 + E\gamma_2, \\ \lambda_2\beta_2 &= F\alpha_2 + B\beta_2 + D\gamma_2, \\ \lambda_2\gamma_2 &= E\alpha_2 + D\beta_2 + C\gamma_2. \end{aligned}$$

Multiplying the first three respectively by α_2, β_2, γ_2 and adding,

16)
$$\begin{aligned} \lambda_1(\alpha_1\alpha_2 + \beta_1\beta_2 + \gamma_1\gamma_2) &= A\alpha_1\alpha_2 + B\beta_1\beta_2 + C\gamma_1\gamma_2 \\ &+ D(\beta_2\gamma_1 + \beta_1\gamma_2) + E(\gamma_2\alpha_1 + \gamma_1\alpha_2) + F(\alpha_2\beta_1 + \alpha_1\beta_2). \end{aligned}$$

If we multiply the second three equations respectively by α_1, β_1, γ_1 and add we obtain for

$$\lambda_2(\alpha_1\alpha_2 + \beta_1\beta_2 + \gamma_1\gamma_2)$$

the same expression. Accordingly we have

17)
$$(\lambda_1 - \lambda_2)(\alpha_1\alpha_2 + \beta_1\beta_2 + \gamma_1\gamma_2) = 0,$$

so that if the roots λ_1, λ_2 are unequal the corresponding axes are perpendicular. In like manner if the determinantal cubic has three unequal roots, the quadric has three mutually perpendicular principal axes.

If two roots are equal the position of the corresponding axes becomes indeterminate, and it may be shown that all radii perpendicular to the direction given by the third root are principal axes of the same length. The surface is then one of revolution about the determinate axis. If all three roots are equal, the surface is a sphere, and any axis is a principal axis.

We will now transform the equation of the quadric 1) to a new set of axes coinciding in direction with its principal axes. Let the new coordinates be x', y', z', and let the direction cosines of the angles made by the new with the old axes be given in the table below.

	x	y	z
x'	α_1	β_1	γ_1
y'	α_2	β_2	γ_2
z'	α_3	β_2	γ_3

The equations of transformation of coordinates are then

18) $$\begin{aligned} x' &= \alpha_1 x + \beta_1 y + \gamma_1 z, \\ y' &= \alpha_2 x + \beta_2 y + \gamma_2 z, \\ z' &= \alpha_3 x + \beta_3 y + \gamma_3 z, \end{aligned}$$

19) $$\begin{aligned} x &= \alpha_1 x' + \alpha_2 y' + \alpha_3 z', \\ y &= \beta_1 x' + \beta_2 y' + \beta_3 z', \\ z &= \gamma_1 x' + \gamma_2 y' + \gamma_3 z'. \end{aligned}$$

Now using equations 19), we obtain

$$\begin{aligned} Ax + Fy + Ez = x'(A\alpha_1 + F\beta_1 + E\gamma_1) \\ + y'(A\alpha_2 + F\beta_2 + E\gamma_2) \\ + z'(A\alpha_3 + F\beta_3 + E\gamma_3), \end{aligned}$$

which in virtue of equations 15) is equal to

$$\lambda_1 \alpha_1 x' + \lambda_2 \alpha_2 y' + \lambda_3 \alpha_3 z'.$$

In like manner

$$\begin{aligned} Fx + By + Dz &= \lambda_1 \beta_1 x' + \lambda_2 \beta_2 y' + \lambda_3 \beta_3 z', \\ Ex + Dy + Cz &= \lambda_1 \gamma_1 x' + \lambda_2 \gamma_2 y' + \lambda_3 \gamma_3 z'. \end{aligned}$$

Multiplying respectively by x, y, z and adding, we obtain

$$Ax^2 + By^2 + Cz^2 + 2Dyz + 2Ezx + 2Fxy$$
$$= \lambda_1 x'(\alpha_1 x + \beta_1 y + \gamma_1 z) + \lambda_2 y'(\alpha_2 x + \beta_2 y + \gamma_2 z) + \lambda_3 z'(\alpha_3 x + \beta_3 y + \gamma_3 z)$$
$$= \lambda_1 x'^2 + \lambda_2 y'^2 + \lambda_3 z'^2.$$

Consequently the equation of the quadric referred to its principal axes is

20) $$\lambda_1 x'^2 + \lambda_2 y'^2 + \lambda_3 z'^2 = 1,$$

and the three roots of the cubic are equal to the squares of the reciprocals of the lengths of the semi-axes. Accordingly in order to find the equation referred to the axes it is not necessary to solve the linear equations 5), but only to solve the cubic 6).

NOTE V.

TRANSFORMATION OF QUADRATIC FORMS.

The last two notes have dealt with quadratic forms, and in Note IV we have by a linear transformation of the variables 19) transformed the form F into a form 20) in which no product terms appear, and we find that the coefficients of the squares are the roots of the determinant 6). In this note we shall consider similar transformations of forms of any number of variables, and shall incidentally obtain a proof of the reality of the roots of Lagrange's determinant, 65), page 159, for the case of no dissipation.

We shall require a number of elementary properties of both linear and quadratic forms, which we shall now set forth. Suppose we have n linear forms

1) $$\begin{aligned} u_1 &= a_{11}x_1 + a_{12}x_2 + \cdots + a_{1n}x_n, \\ u_2 &= a_{21}x_1 + a_{22}x_2 + \cdots + a_{2n}x_n, \\ & \cdots\cdots\cdots\cdots\cdots\cdots \\ & \cdots\cdots\cdots\cdots\cdots\cdots \\ u_n &= a_{n1}x_1 + a_{n2}x_2 + \cdots + a_{nn}x_n, \end{aligned}$$

and let us call R the determinant

2) $$R = \begin{vmatrix} a_{11}, & a_{12}, & \dots & a_{1n} \\ a_{21}, & a_{22}, & \dots & a_{2n} \\ \cdot & \cdot & \cdot & \cdot \\ a_{n1}, & a_{n2}, & \dots & a_{nn} \end{vmatrix}.$$

If we multiply the kth column of R by x_k, and then add to this column the first, second, etc., multiplied respectively by $x_1, x_2, \dots,$ we obtain

3) $$Rx_k = \begin{vmatrix} a_{11}, & \dots & a_{1,k-1}, & u_1, & a_{1,k+1}, & \dots & a_{1n} \\ a_{21}, & \dots & a_{2,k-1}, & u_2, & a_{2,k+1}, & \dots & a_{2n} \\ \cdot & \cdot & \cdot & \cdot & \cdot & \cdot & \cdot \\ a_{n1}, & \dots & a_{n,k-1}, & u_n, & a_{n,k+1}, & \dots & a_{nn} \end{vmatrix}.$$

If now the determinant R is zero, the determinant on the right vanishes, expanding which we obtain

4) $$c_1u_1 + c_2u_2 + \cdots + c_nu_n = 0,$$

where the c's are the minors of the elements of the kth column of R. Thus if the determinant of the forms vanishes, the forms are not independent, but satisfy identically the linear relation 4).

Consider now the quadratic form

5) $$f(x_1, x_2 \dots x_n) = \sum_{r=1}^{r=n}\sum_{s=1}^{s=n} a_{rs}x_rx_s,$$

for which $a_{rs} = a_{sr}$, and

$$6)\qquad u_r = \frac{1}{2}\frac{\partial f}{\partial x_r} = \frac{1}{2} f_r' = \sum_{s=1}^{s=n} a_{rs} x_s,$$

$$7)\qquad f = \frac{1}{2}\sum_{r=1}^{r=n} f_r' x_r = \sum_{r=1}^{r=n} u_r x_r.$$

If $y_1, y_2, \ldots y_n$ are another set of variables, and we put for each x_r the value $x_r + \lambda y_r$ we have

$$f(x_1 + \lambda y_1, \ldots x_n + \lambda y_n) = \sum_{r=1}^{r=n}\sum_{s=1}^{s=n} a_{rs}(x_r + \lambda y_r)(x_s + \lambda y_s)$$

$$8)\qquad = \sum_{r=1}^{r=n}\sum_{s=1}^{s=n} a_{rs} x_r x_s + 2\lambda \sum_{r=1}^{r=n}\sum_{s=1}^{s=n} a_{rs} x_r y_s + \lambda^2 \sum_{r=1}^{r=n}\sum_{s=1}^{s=n} a_{rs} y_r y_s$$

$$= f(x_1, \ldots x_n) + \lambda \sum_{r=1}^{r=n} f_r'(x) y_r + \lambda^2 f(y_1, \ldots y_n).$$

If now R, the *determinant of the form* f vanishes, we have a relation

$$9)\qquad c_1 u_1 + c_2 u_2 + \cdots + c_n u_n \equiv \frac{1}{2}\sum_{r=1}^{r=n} c_r f_r'(x_1, \ldots x_n) = 0$$

for *all* values of $x_1, \ldots x_n$.

Let us now put for the y's of equation 8) the values of c of equation 9). We then have by 7) and 9)

$$f(c_1, \ldots c_n) = \frac{1}{2}\sum_{r=1}^{r=n} c_r f_r'(c_1, \ldots c_n) = 0,$$

so that 8) becomes

$$10)\qquad \begin{aligned} f(x_1 + \lambda c_1, \ldots x_n + \lambda c_n) &= f(x_1, \ldots x_n) \\ + \lambda \sum_{r=1}^{r=n} c_r f_r'(x_1, \ldots x_n) &= f(x_1, \ldots x_n). \end{aligned}$$

We thus find that in this case f is independent of λ and of $y_1, \ldots y_n$. Accordingly if c_n is not zero, let us put $\lambda = -\frac{x_n}{c_n}$, so that we obtain for all values of $x_1, \ldots x_n$,

$$11)\qquad f(x_1, \ldots x_n) = f\left(x_1 - \frac{c_1}{c_n} x_n,\ x_2 - \frac{c_2}{c_n} x_n, \ldots x_{n-1} - \frac{c_{n-1}}{c_n} x_n,\ 0\right).$$

Thus we obtain the theorem: every quadratic form in n variables whose determinant vanishes, may be expressed as a quadratic form of *less* than n other variables y, which are linear combinations of the original

variables. Such forms are called *singular,* as opposed to *ordinary* forms, whose determinant does not vanish. As an example the form

$$x_1^2 + x_2^2 - x_3^2 + 2\,x_1 x_2,$$

whose determinant

$$\begin{vmatrix} 1 & 1 & 0 \\ 1 & 1 & 0 \\ 0 & 0 & -1 \end{vmatrix}$$

vanishes, may be written

$$(x_1 + x_2 + x_3)(x_1 + x_2 - x_3).$$

If f is an ordinary form and a_{rr} is not zero, we may write

12) $$f = a_{rr} x_r^2 + 2\,x_r p + q,$$

where p is a linear form containing all the other variables except x_r and q is a quadratic form in the same variables. Completing the square we may then write

13) $$a_{rr} f = (a_{rr} x_r + p)^2 + a_{rr}\, q - p^2.$$

If on the other hand every coefficient of a square a_{rr} is zero, we may write

14) $$f = 2\,a_{rs} x_r x_s + 2\,x_r p + 2\,x_s q + r,$$

where p, q are linear, r a quadratic form not containing either x_r or x_s, we may then write

15) $$\begin{aligned} 2\,a_{rs} f &= 4(a_{rs} x_r + q)(a_{rs} x_s + p) + 2\,a_{rs} r - 4\,pq \\ &= \{a_{rs}(x_r + x_s) + p + q\}^2 - \{a_{rs}(x_r - x_s) - p + q\}^2 + 2\,a_{rs} r - 4\,pq. \end{aligned}$$

In the former case we have exhibited f as the sum of a square and a form in $n - 1$ variables, in the latter as two terms in squares and a form in $n - 2$ variables. In either case the remaining form may be treated in a similar manner, and so on, so that the form is eventually reduced to a sum of terms in squares. If the coefficients A of all the squares in

16) $$f = A_1 y_1^2 + A_2 y_2^2 \cdots + A_n y_n^2,$$

when the y's are linear forms in $x_1, \ldots x_n$, have the same sign, the form is said to be *definite*, for it can not change sign however the values of the variables be altered. If the coefficients A are not all of the same sign the form is indefinite.

If we transform the linear forms 1) by means of the linear substitution

17) $$\begin{aligned} x_1 &= \beta_{11} y_1 + \beta_{12} y_2 + \cdots + \beta_{1n} y_n, \\ x_2 &= \beta_{21} y_1 + \beta_{22} y_2 + \cdots + \beta_{2n} y_n, \\ &\ldots\ldots\ldots\ldots\ldots\ldots \\ x_n &= \beta_{n1} y_1 + \beta_{n2} y_2 + \cdots + \beta_{nn} y_n, \end{aligned}$$

we obtain linear forms in the new variables $y_1, \dots y_n$, so that if we write

18)
$$\begin{aligned} u_1 &= c_{11} y_1 + c_{12} y_2 + \cdots + c_{1n} y_n, \\ u_2 &= c_{21} y_1 + c_{22} y_2 + \cdots + c_{2n} y_n, \\ &\cdots\cdots\cdots\cdots \\ u_n &= c_{n1} y_1 + c_{n2} y_2 + \cdots + c_{nn} y_n, \end{aligned}$$

we find by carrying out the transformation,

19)
$$c_{rs} = \sum_{t=1}^{t=n} a_{rt} \beta_{ts}.$$

But this is, according to the rule for multiplication of two determinants the condition that the determinant of the forms u in y,

20)
$$\begin{vmatrix} c_{11}, \dots c_{1n} \\ \cdots\cdots \\ \cdots\cdots \\ c_{n1}, \dots c_{nn} \end{vmatrix} = \begin{vmatrix} a_{11}, \dots a_{1n} \\ \cdots\cdots \\ \cdots\cdots \\ a_{n1}, \dots a_{nn} \end{vmatrix} \begin{vmatrix} \beta_{11}, \dots \beta_{1n} \\ \cdots\cdots \\ \cdots\cdots \\ \beta_{n1}, \dots \beta_{nn} \end{vmatrix}$$

is the product of the determinant of the forms in x by the determinant of the substitution 17).

The determinant in which the element in the rth row and s^{th} column is a derivative $\frac{\partial u_r}{\partial x_s}$ is called the Jacobian of the functions $u_1, \dots u_n$ with respect to the variables $x_1, \dots x_n$, and is often denoted by

$$\frac{\partial(u_1, \dots u_n)}{\partial(x_1, \dots x_n)}.$$

In this notation 20) becomes

21)
$$\frac{\partial(u_1, \dots u_n)}{\partial(y_1, \dots y_n)} = \frac{\partial(u_1, \dots u_n)}{\partial(x_1, \dots x_n)} \begin{vmatrix} \beta_{11}, \dots \beta_{1n} \\ \cdots\cdots \\ \beta_{n1}, \dots \beta_{nn} \end{vmatrix}.$$

If the functions $u_1, \dots u_n$ in a Jacobian are the partial derivatives of the same function f, $u_r = \frac{\partial f}{\partial x_r}$, so that the element in the rth row and s^{th} column is $\frac{\partial^2 f}{\partial x_r \partial x_s}$ the determinant is called the Hessian of the function. Thus the determinant R of 2) is the Hessian of f, and will be denoted by $H_x f$.

If now we transform the quadratic form 5) by the substitution 17), so that

22)
$$f = \sum_{r=1}^{r=n} \sum_{s=1}^{s=n} a_{rs} x_r x_s = \sum_{r=1}^{r=n} \sum_{s=1}^{s=n} A_{rs} y_r y_s,$$

we may find a relation between the Hessians of f with respect to the x's and that with respect to the y's. Using the notation for Jacobians, by 21),

$$23)\quad H_y f = \frac{\partial\left(\frac{\partial f}{\partial y_1}, \dots \frac{\partial f}{\partial y_n}\right)}{\partial(y_1, \dots y_n)} = \frac{\partial\left(\frac{\partial f}{\partial y_1}, \dots \frac{\partial f}{\partial y_n}\right)}{\partial(x_1, \dots x_n)} \begin{vmatrix} \beta_{11}, \dots \beta_{1n} \\ \dots\dots \\ \dots\dots \\ \beta_{n1}, \dots \beta_{nn} \end{vmatrix}.$$

But in every derivative

$$\frac{\partial^2 f}{\partial x_r \partial y_s} = \frac{\partial^2 f}{\partial y_s \partial x_r} = \frac{\partial u_r}{\partial y_s}.$$

Consequently the Jacobian on the right of 23) is the same as that on the *left* of 21).

Thus we find

$$24)\qquad H_y f = \frac{\partial(u_1 \dots u_n)}{\partial(x_1 \dots x_n)} \begin{vmatrix} \beta_{11} \dots \beta_{1n} \\ \dots\dots \\ \beta_{n1} \dots \beta_{nn} \end{vmatrix}^2 = H_x f \begin{vmatrix} \beta_{11} \dots \beta_{1n} \\ \dots\dots \\ \beta_{n1} \dots \beta_{nn} \end{vmatrix}^2$$

or the determinant of the transformed form is equal to that of the original form multiplied by the square of the determinant of transformation.

If an ordinary form f vanishes for a particular set of values

$$x_1 = c_1, \quad x_2 = c_2 \dots x_n = c_n,$$

where the c's are not all zero, we can show that the form is indefinite. For if we substitute for the x's excepting x_n, the values

$$25)\quad x_1 = c_1 \frac{x_n}{c_n} + y_1, \; x_2 = c_2 \frac{x_n}{c_n} + y_2, \dots x_{n-1} = c_{n-1} \frac{x_n}{c_n} + y_{n-1},$$

we have

$$f = \sum_{r=1}^{r=n} \sum_{s=1}^{s=n} a_{rs} x_r x_s = \sum_{r=1}^{r=n-1} \sum_{s=1}^{s=n-1} a_{rs} \left(c_r \frac{x_n}{c_n} + y_r\right)\left(c_s \frac{x_n}{c_n} + y_s\right)$$

$$26)\qquad + x_n \sum_{s=1}^{s=n-1} a_{sn}\left(c_s \frac{x_n}{c_n} + y_s\right) + a_{nn} x_n^2$$

$$= \frac{x_n^2}{c_n^2} \sum_{r=1}^{r=n} \sum_{s=1}^{s=n} a_{rs} c_r c_s + \frac{2x_n}{c_n} \sum_{r=1}^{r=n} \sum_{s=1}^{s=n-1} a_{rs} c_r y_s + \sum_{r=1}^{r=n-1} \sum_{s=1}^{s=n-1} a_{rs} y_r y_s.$$

The first term, containing $f(c_1, \dots c_n)$ as a factor, vanishes by hypothesis. The sums in the other terms contain only $n-1$ variables. If then there are any values of $y_1, \dots y_{n-1}$, for which $\sum_{r=1}^{r=n} \sum_{s=1}^{s=n-1} a_{rs} c_r y_s$ does not vanish, since x_n is independent of these variables, we may by suitably choosing the value of x_n make the form have either sign, it is therefore indefinite.

(If the sum $\sum_{r=1}^{r=n}\sum_{s=1}^{s=n-1} a_{rs} c_r y_s$ is zero for all values of $y_1, \ldots y_{n-1}$, we must have

$$\sum_{r=1}^{r=n} a_{rs} c_r = 0$$

for $s = 1, 2, , \ldots n-1$, but since $f(c_1, \ldots c_n)$ is zero we must have also $\sum_{r=1}^{r=n} a_{rn} c_r$, and these n equations require the determinant of the form to vanish, and the form is singular.)

As a result of this theorem we see that if a form is to be definite, no coefficient a_{rr} of a square x_r^2 must be absent, and all must have the same sign. For if $a_{rr} = 0$, putting all the variables equal to zero except x_r would make the form vanish, and if a_{rr} is not zero, the same assumption would make the form have the sign of a_{rr}. Consequently all these coefficients must be of the same sign.

Let us now consider two ordinary quadratic forms of the same variables, with real coefficients[1])

$$27)\qquad \varphi = \sum_{r=1}^{r=n}\sum_{s=1}^{s=n} a_{rs} x_r x_s, \quad \psi = \sum_{r=1}^{r=n}\sum_{s=1}^{s=n} c_{rs} x_r x_s,$$

from which with an arbitrary multiplier λ we construct the form

$$28)\qquad \lambda\varphi + \psi.$$

As we give λ an infinite set of real values, we obtain an infinite *sheaf* of forms. Let us examine whether they are definite or not.

The determinant of the form $\lambda\varphi + \psi$

$$28)\qquad \begin{vmatrix} \lambda a_{11} + c_{11}, & \lambda a_{12} + c_{12}, & \ldots \lambda a_{1n} + c_{1n} \\ \lambda a_{21} + c_{21}, & \lambda a_{22} + c_{22}, & \ldots \lambda a_{2n} + c_{2n} \\ \cdots & \cdots & \cdots \\ \cdots & \cdots & \cdots \\ \lambda a_{n1} + c_{n1}, & \lambda a_{n2} + c_{n2}, & \ldots \lambda a_{nn} + c_{nn} \end{vmatrix} = f(\lambda)$$

is identical with Lagrange's determinant, page 159, when the $\varkappa$'s are zero. (We here have written λ for the λ^2 on p. 159.) We shall now prove that if the equation $f(\lambda) = 0$ has a complex root, all the forms of the sheaf $\lambda\varphi + \psi$ are indefinite.

Let $\lambda = \alpha + i\beta$ be a complex root of the determinantal equation $f(\lambda) = 0$. Then since the form $(\alpha + i\beta)\varphi + \psi$ is singular, it may be represented as a sum of less than n squares, and since it is complex, these may be squares of complex variables, so that we have

$$29)\qquad (\alpha + i\beta)\varphi + \psi = (y_1 + iz_1)^2 + (y_2 + iz_2)^2 + \cdots + (y_{n-1} + iz_{n-1})^2,$$

1) Kronecker, *Über Schaaren quadratischer Formen.* Monatsber. der Königl. Preuß. Akad. d. Wiss. zu Berlin, 1868. pp. 339—346. Werke, Bd. I, p. 165.

the y's and z's being real linear forms in the x's, any of which, but not all, may be zero. Separating the real and the imaginary terms, we obtain

30) $$\alpha\varphi + \psi = \sum_{r=1}^{r=n-1}(y_r^2 - z_r^2), \quad \beta\varphi = 2\sum_{r=1}^{r=n-1} y_r z_r.$$

From the two forms

31) $$\sum_{r=1}^{r=n-1}(y_r^2 - z_r^2), \quad \sum_{r=1}^{r=n-1} y_r z_r$$

the whole sheaf may be obtained. Solving 30) for φ and ψ,

32) $$\lambda\varphi + \psi = \sum_{r=1}^{r=n-1}(y_r^2 - z_r^2) + \frac{2(\lambda-\alpha)}{\beta}\sum_{r=1}^{r=n-1} y_r z_r,$$

which we may write

33) $$\lambda\varphi + \psi = \sum_{r=1}^{r=n-1}(y_r - \mu z_r)\left(y_r + \frac{1}{\mu} z_r\right),$$

where

$$\frac{1}{\mu} - \mu = \frac{2(\lambda-\alpha)}{\beta},$$

a quadratic in μ, giving for every real value of λ a real value of μ. Now each of the forms 33) vanishes for values of $x_1, \ldots x_n$ other than zero, which satisfy the $n-1$ linear equations

34) $$0 = y_1 - \mu z_1 = y_2 - \mu z_2 = \cdots = y_{n-1} - \mu z_{n-1},$$

and is accordingly indefinite. Conversely if there is in the sheaf a single definite form, the roots of $f(\lambda) = 0$ are all real. Now in the mechanical application, the form φ, which is proportional to that given by the value $\lambda = \infty$, is the kinetic energy, a definite positive form, consequently the reality of the roots is proved.

If $\lambda_\varkappa$ is one of the real roots of the equation $f(\lambda) = 0$ the form $\lambda_\varkappa\varphi + \psi$ being singular, can be expressed in terms of less than n linear functions of $x_1, \ldots x_n$, say $y_1, \ldots y_{n-1}$. Let y_n be any other linear function of the x's, such that the determinant of the functions $y_1, \ldots y_n$ is not zero, then we can express the function φ in terms of these n variables y, and if it is definite and positive, the coefficient of every square will have a positive sign, accordingly, as in 12), 13), we may separate off from φ a square $z_\varkappa^2$, where z contains y_n, and accordingly we have

35) $$\begin{aligned}\lambda\varphi + \psi &= (\lambda - \lambda_\varkappa)\varphi + \lambda_\varkappa\varphi + \psi \\ &= (\lambda - \lambda_\varkappa) z_\varkappa^2 + \lambda\varphi' + \psi',\end{aligned}$$

where $\lambda\varphi' + \psi'$ contains only the $n-1$ variables $y_1, \ldots y_{n-1}$. Now a definite form in n variables remains a definite form in $n-1$ variables if we put any variable equal to zero, consequently φ' is, like φ, a definite positive form.

A linear divisor such as $\lambda - \lambda_r$ of the determinant of the form $\lambda\varphi' + \psi'$ is also a divisor of the determinant of $\lambda\varphi + \psi$, for on writing out the determinant of the form 35) in terms of $y_1, \dots y_{n-1}, z_\varkappa$, we find

$$36)\quad H_{z_\varkappa, y_1, \dots y_{n-1}}(\lambda\varphi + \psi) = (\lambda - \lambda_\varkappa) H_{y_1, \dots y_{n-1}}(\lambda\varphi' + \psi'),$$

so that the vanishing of the determinant of order $n - 1$ on the right makes the determinant on the left vanish. But this equal to the determinant of $\lambda\varphi + \psi$ in the variables $x_1, \dots x_n$ multiplied by a constant.

We may now treat the form $\lambda\varphi' + \psi'$ in the same manner, and so on, so that finally we obtain

$$37)\quad \lambda\varphi + \psi = (\lambda - \lambda_1)z_1^2 + (\lambda - \lambda_2)z_2^2 + \dots + (\lambda - \lambda_n)z_n^2,$$

where $\lambda_1, \dots \lambda_n$ are the roots of the determinantal equation $f(\lambda) = 0$. Since this is true for all values of λ we have

$$38)\quad \begin{aligned} \varphi &= z_1^2 + z_2^2 + \dots + z_n^2, \\ -\psi &= \lambda_1 z_1^2 + \lambda_2 z_2^2 + \dots + \lambda_n z_n^2, \end{aligned}$$

which is the simultaneous transformation of two quadratic forms required in the treatment of principal coordinates. It is obvious according to this method that it makes no difference whether the determinant has equal roots or not.

INDEX.

(The numbers refer to pages.)

ERRATA. ✓

p. 30, line 21, for $\gamma = 6.576$ read $\gamma = 6.6576$.
„ 205, line 7 from bottom, for AB and PQ read AP and BQ.

Printed by B. G. Teubner, Dresden.

Printed in Dunstable, United Kingdom

91342465R00338